Suzi Castle's

Deliciously Healthy
Favorite Foods Cookbook

"I have read and tried some of the recipes in this cookbook, and I would recommend it to my patients. It is an outstanding low-fat, low-calorie cookbook."

Rabinder S. Bhogal, M.D., Gastroenterology and Liver Diseases

"In 16 years of eating a heart-healthy diet, I have acquired quite a few cookbooks. I look forward to adding this book to my collection—it's up-to-date, easy to read, factual and interesting. I appreciate the recipes' ease of preparation and the use of on-hand ingredients."

Laura Brockmeyer, newsletter editor, The Mended Hearts, Inc.

"I find the theory behind this cookbook to be a sound approach based on traditional data. The recipes are easy to follow, varied and include many of our favorite foods; the user of his healthy eating program will neither become bored nor feel deprived. The adjustments to our eating habits are reasonable and should not necessitate an increase in the food budget. With this program, it will no longer be necessary to prepare two meals, one for the user and one for the rest of the family."

Leo Costa, Jr., author and fitness expert

"As people become more health-conscious, this book will become an invaluable part of both the health professional's and home cook's library."

Patrick D. Daley, M.D., Family Practice, Sports and Bariatric Medicine

"By adopting the dietary guidelines behind the recipes in this book, people may significantly reduce their risk of diet-related cardiovascular disease. With obesity, diabetes and coronary artery disease reaching epidemic proportions in America, it's high time we returned to the healthful eating habits that our bodies were designed for."

Richard Heiss, M.D., Family Practice

"This book is a must for everyone seeking a healthy way of eating. Recently I have been trying to cut as much fat and calories out of my diet as possible, and that's where this book caught my attention. I tried several of the recipes and found them both delicious and easy to prepare. The hints in the front of the book were very helpful and informative."

Denise Leeth, owner, *Senior Advocate Newspaper*

"I am pleased to endorse this cookbook. Our diet needs more emphasis on fiber, fruit and vegetables. Fiber reduces the incidence of gastrointestinal disorders such as diverticulitis, and it helps in lowering cholesterol."

Anil Mehta, M.D., Gastroenterology and Liver Diseases

"Life-style change is difficult for all of us. Tools like this book, which make changes seem not only possible but easily accomplished, are very valuable. This book should be in every kitchen."

Jean Palmer-Daley, Ph.D., Marriage, Family and Child Therapist

Suzi Castle's

Deliciously Healthy
Favorite Foods Cookbook

Health Cookbooks

Health Cookbooks
Rt. 4, Box 208
Porterville, CA 93257-9708

Copyright ©1996 by Suzi Castle
First Printing 1996
Printed in the United States of America

Publisher's Cataloging in Publication
   Castle, Suzi
Suzi Castle's deliciously healthy favorite foods cookbook. —
Porterville, Calif. : Health Cookbooks, 1996.
   p. cm.
   Includes index.
   ISBN 0-9647423-2-2

   1. Cookery.   2. Nutrition.   3. Low-fat diet—Recipes.
4. Sugar-free diet—Recipes.   I. Title.

TX651.C38 1996   641.5'63
                                              QBI95-20377

Library of Congress Catalog Number: 95-94689

Thanks to my many friends and co-workers, whose help and encouragement made this book a reality. Including:

Book Design: Christine Nolt, Cirrus Design

Cover Design: Itoko Maeno

Copy Editing: Nancy Capelle

Indexing: Nancy Freedom, Freedom Workshop

Production Consultants: Carolyn Porter and Alan Gadney, One on One Designs

Business Consultant: Mike DePetro, DePetro & Associates

Consulting Dietitian: Joy A. Smith, R.D., C.D.E., calculated the diabetic exchanges for the recipes. The basis for her calculation was the nutrient analysis provided by the author. "It is hoped that providing the exchange values will enable those who have meal patterns to incorporate these exciting recipes into them. In some cases, the fat content is so low that part or all of a fat exchange will need to be added to the meal at which the recipe is used. This is noted on each recipe as deemed necessary. Bon Appétit."

*Dedicated to all the good cooks
in my family, who were
my inspiration.*

Contents

Introduction

With the *Deliciously Healthy Favorite Foods Cookbook*, you will discover how easy it is to eat healthy versions of your favorite foods. We all know that a low-fat diet will help us stay slim and healthy. Yet none of us want to give up the good taste of our favorite "comfort" foods—like hamburgers, brownies, pizza, fried chicken, clam chowder and potato chips.

The *Deliciously Healthy Favorite Foods Cookbook* offers low-fat, sugar-free versions of the foods you love to eat. Each recipe has a nutritional analysis that lists the calories, fats, fiber, carbohydrates, sodium, protein and cholesterol for each serving. For persons with diabetes, a registered dietitian has calculated food exchanges. You'll find a wonderful variety of recipes— everything from appetizers to desserts.

A healthy, well-balanced diet can increase your energy level and feeling of well-being and add many vigorous years to your life. That's where the *Deliciously Healthy Favorite Foods Cookbook* can make a delicious difference. The easy recipes offer maximum taste with minimum fuss—a perfect combination for today's busy life-styles and discriminating tastes. You will learn healthier cooking methods, shopping skills and how to adapt your own favorite recipes. Turning ordinary foods into extraordinary meals is easier than you ever imagined!

Choosing to eat and cook "healthy" is a priority that will have lifelong rewards. Set realistic goals, and make the small, achievable changes in your diet that will allow you to lose weight and improve your health. When making a decision to change unhealthy habits, always view these changes as "easy," and they will become so. No one else can make these decisions and changes for you. So make a commitment to treat yourself better, and before long it will become second nature. You'll find that you will have new energy, self-confidence and self-esteem. You can do it!

Eating right is easier than many people realize. Simply cut down on fats, sugars and salt and increase your consumption of whole grains, vegetables and fruits. Eating a variety of foods improves nutrition and increases eating satisfaction. With whole foods, which are naturally high in fiber and low in fat, it's easier to feel full on relatively few calories. If you stick to such low-fat foods, you can let your appetite tell you when to stop eating. Not only will you feel less deprived, but you'll be protecting yourself against the diseases that have been linked to the typical American diet, such as heart disease, hypertension, some cancers and diabetes. With the *Deliciously Healthy Favorite Foods Cookbook*, you will love eating "healthy."

Helpful Hints

To make your new, healthier eating plan even easier, the following tips and techniques will help you win the "battle of the bulge" and get good-for-you meals on the table fast.

Prepared mixes and ingredients, if low in fat, sugar and sodium, can be valuable time-savers in preparing quick, healthy meals.

Food labels. Use the new nutritional labels on packaged foods to help you make wise decisions on which products to choose. One reason people eat too much fat, sugar and salt is that they don't know what they are eating.

Thirsty or hungry? Often thirst is misinterpreted as hunger. Drink plenty of water (six to eight glasses daily) to keep from snacking.

Educate your palate to prefer low-fat foods. When you substitute well-seasoned and properly prepared foods, fat no longer plays an important role in achieving flavor.

Watch out for hidden calories in condiments. Learn to use mustard instead of mayonnaise on sandwiches. Spread sugar-free jam instead of butter on your morning bagel. Beware of high-fat dressings and toppings at the salad bar. Hidden fats can sabotage a weight loss plan.

Have a snack! Planned, measured between-meal snacks can give you extra energy and alertness while keeping your appetite down. If you go too many hours without eating, you will be more likely to overeat at your next meal. Keep a good supply of healthy snack foods such as fresh fruits, vegetable sticks, fat-free crackers, unsalted pretzels and air-popped popcorn for when you're feeling "munchy."

Learn to season. Become a connoisseur of spices and herbs to turn low-calorie meals into fine cuisine. Use fresh lemon or lime juice, fat-free broth, herbs, spices and small amounts of wine for flavor instead of relying on salt, sugar and fat.

Keep a food diary. To become more aware of all foods eaten, it's helpful to keep a food diary. Better yet, write down what you intend to eat, including sensible snacks. This plan will offer important guidance when you are tempted by foods not on your diet. A log can identify what you are doing to sabotage your healthy eating plan. Learn to make calories count for good nutrition.

Practice portion control. Take pleasure in every bite, and savor the flavor by eating more slowly. By choosing sensible portions, you can allow yourself to eat foods that once were "forbidden."

Don't skip meals—especially breakfast. People who skip meals tend to overeat later in the day. A drop in blood sugar levels can leave you feeling weak and ravenously hungry. It's best to eat regular meals, even if they are small ones.

Eat more complex carbohydrates. Foods high in complex carbohydrates and low in fat, such as fresh fruits and vegetables, cereal, rice, pasta and legumes, can satisfy the appetite with fewer calories. Carbohydrates should be the major source of energy in your diet—60 to 70 percent of daily calories. Most starchy foods are almost fat-free. Carbohydrates are great for weight control because your body burns more calories metabolizing them than it does metabolizing fat. They will keep your hunger at bay longer because they stabilize your blood sugar levels. You will have less desire for fat, sugar and excess protein—the main culprits of weight gain.

Shopping tips. Limit your purchases to low-fat or fat-free ingredients. Don't take home foods that might tempt you to go off your diet plan. Substitute lower-fat cuts of meat; choose nonfat or low-fat (1%) milk and cheeses.

Discover the huge array of healthy products that are now available. Don't be fooled by foods labeled "lite," for many are still loaded with calories. Don't shop when you are hungry. You might be tempted to purchase foods that you shouldn't. Make a list and stick to it!

Feast on fiber. Because foods that are fiber-rich need more chewing than other foods, they're perfect for slowing down your eating. Eating more slowly helps you to eat less. Foods high in fiber (but low in fats and sugars) tend to have fewer calories than less-fiber-rich foods. They are more filling as well, which leaves you feeling more satisfied. Soluble fiber, found in beans, apples, carrots and potatoes, also helps to keep insulin levels lower after a meal. A high-fiber diet helps to control weight gain, cuts down on fat absorption during digestion, lowers blood cholesterol, helps to keep blood pressure down and discourages bowel cancer.

Cooking Tips

Learn how to "lighten" your favorite recipes. Experiment by cutting down on fats, salt and sugar. Be sure to write down the changes you have made. These notes will help with further recipe adjustments.

> **Cut the fat**. Yet keep the great flavor. Never fry in oil. Nonstick sprays are easy to use and produce excellent results for broiling, grilling, stir-frying, steaming, baking, roasting and microwaving. When reducing the fat in, or eliminating the fat from, baked goods, substitute an equal amount of unsweetened applesauce or nonfat yogurt. Remove fat from soups and gravies by first chilling to congeal the fat. Or use a fat separator, an inexpensive cup with a spout at the bottom, that allows you to pour off the lean broth underneath and leave the fat at the top behind.

> **Use "light" cooking methods**. Choose cooking methods that help remove fat, such as baking, broiling, barbecuing, roasting, stewing and steaming.

> **Oven-roasting and frying**. To create the flavor and crunchiness of fried foods without adding any fat, roast meats and vegetables at 400° to 500°. Place food in a large, heavy skillet sprayed with nonstick spray. Food should be in a single layer. Do not crowd. Roast until golden brown and cooked through. Oven-roasting produces a crispy, browned outer crust, concentrates flavors and creates delicious aromas to add to eating pleasure.

> **"Steam-sauté."** Place vegetables, cut into bite-size pieces, in a heavy skillet sprayed with nonstick spray. Stir-fry over medium to high heat, but cover occasionally if vegetables become too dry. Cook until crisp-tender.

> **Plan ahead**. Coordination and planning will simplify and speed up meal preparation. Keep a good supply of healthy canned goods in your pantry, including cooked beans, fish, vegetables, poultry, prepared mixes and sauces.

Cooking ahead saves time, money and energy. When you have healthy foods already prepared, the temptation to grab a quick, but less healthy, meal is reduced. When you're away from home, it's smart to take food with you, such as fresh fruit or a low-fat snack. That way you won't be tempted to eat whatever happens to be around, such as candy bars or fast food.

Visual appeal. It's true that we eat with our eyes as well as our mouths. Artful presentation makes food look more attractive and seem more delicious. The easiest way to bring a dish to life is to use garnishes, which offer a color contrast. Often a simple sprig of parsley is most effective. Let your creativity concoct a visual feast.

Ingredients

Fruits and vegetables. Choose only the freshest produce available. In addition to being more nutritious, fresh fruits and vegetables are also more flavorful. You won't need to add fatty sauces or butter. Your supermarket salad bar can be a wonderful time-saver. You easily can pick up the ingredients for a healthy salad or stir-fry.

Poultry. Remove all visible fat and skin. Boneless cuts are the easiest and fastest to prepare. Be aware that some ground poultry may not be as lean as you expect, because skin may have been added. Ask your butcher to custom-grind skinless white meat, or grind your own in a food processor. When poaching chicken breasts, cook extra and freeze. These can be used later for quick additions to salads, soups, sandwiches or casserole dishes.

Fish. Most fish and shellfish are healthy and low-fat. Always choose low-fat methods of preparation, and don't drench them with butter or high-fat sauces. Purchase only water-packed tuna and drain well to remove excess sodium.

Meats. Eaten in moderation, lean meats won't "blow" your fat budget. Choose well-trimmed cuts with no marbling. Trim off any visible fat. Best cuts include tenderloin, sirloin, round and flank.

Dried legumes. Beans, lentils and split peas are probably your best buys in the supermarket. They're loaded with protein, rich in fiber and nutrients, inexpensive, fat-free and low in calories. (If your busy schedule doesn't allow time to cook dried legumes, use canned versions.) They are often more filling than other foods and tend to leave a person feeling more satisfied after a meal. Plan to serve vegetarian entrées several times a week.

Nonfat milk powder. Nonfat milk powder is convenient to use, because it is always fresh and available when you need it. It is low in calories, rich in nutrients and less expensive than fresh milk. A double-strength mixture of nonfat or very low-fat (½%) milk powder is an excellent substitute for cream in recipes.

Dairy products. Choose only very low-fat or nonfat milk, yogurt, sour cream and cheeses. New, improved versions come out every day, and many are amazingly rich in taste. Conveniently packaged grated fat-free cheeses are a great time-saver for busy cooks. New fat-free margarine means that you can spread it guilt-free.

Brown rice. For a nutty flavor, appealing color and faster cooking time, first toast brown rice by stir-frying in a dry, heavy skillet until golden, and then cook according to recipe directions.

Nuts and seeds. Toasting seeds and nuts in a dry skillet over medium heat accentuates flavor and adds an attractive golden color. Since nuts and seeds are very high in fat, only small quantities are allowed on a low-fat diet. They are best used sparingly as a garnish.

Sugar substitutes. Sugar gives you a quick energy boost, followed by an energy letdown, which leaves you feeling more hungry than ever. Sugar adds "empty" calories that contribute little toward good nutrition. To eliminate sugar from your cooking, consider using sugar substitutes equal to the amount of sugar called for in a recipe. (See the package for an equivalence chart.) You may choose to use more or less, according to your personal preference. Experiment with different types of sweeteners to achieve the results you desire. *Aspartame sweeteners* (i.e., Equal®) have a superior sweetening ability but break down if baked or heated too long. For some recipes, they can be added after the cooking process. They are well suited to foods that don't need to be cooked, such as gelatin or fruit. *Saccharin sweeteners* (i.e., SugarTwin® and Sweet'N Low®) do not break down with heat and are recommended for cooking methods that require longer exposure to heat.

Flour. To add more fiber and nutrients to your recipes, use ½ unbleached flour and ½ whole wheat flour in place of bleached flour. Whole wheat pastry flour produces lighter results for baked goods.

Eggs. Egg whites are a healthy source of protein, but cholesterol-laden yolks should be limited to three or four a week, and that includes those used for baking. Use one egg plus two egg whites instead of two whole eggs. Or use ¼ cup fat-free or low-fat egg substitute for each whole egg called for.

Seasonings

Let your taste buds be your guide. Be creative with new seasonings, to add flavor but keep calories down.

Chicken stock. Add rich, buttery flavor to soups, vegetables, sauces and stews by adding chicken stock or chicken bouillon granules. If you are on a salt-restricted diet, choose the low-sodium varieties available.

Butter-flavored granules. Very low in fat, sodium and calories, butter-flavored granules add rich flavor to baked goods, sauces and soups. Sprinkle them over hot, cooked foods for a delicious, buttery taste.

Use salt in moderation. Excess salt can contribute to high blood pressure and heart disease. It's best to limit salt to 1,500 to 2,500 milligrams a day. Beware of processed foods, like pickles, bacon, ham, canned soups and snack chips, which contribute 75 percent of the sodium in the average diet. Keep the salt shaker off the table and choose "lite" salt in place of regular salt when cooking. Learn to season with lemon or lime juice, wine, herbs, spices and vegetable juices.

Seasoned vinegars. Make your own herb vinegar by adding a tablespoon of fresh herbs to a cup of vinegar. Allow flavors to blend for a few days before using. Strain off herbs and serve in an attractive cruet.

Use aromatics. To heighten flavor, use onions, leeks and garlic to season your food. They are especially delicious when gently sautéed in a skillet sprayed with nonstick spray.

Flavored oils. A small amount of flavorful oil, such as extra-virgin olive oil or sesame oil, lends a lot of flavor without adding many calories.

Helpful Kitchen Equipment

Food processor. A great time-saver, capable of slicing, grating, chopping, grinding or simply mixing.

Blender. Convenient for mixing, liquifying and pureeing. Most effective if food is cut into chunks before adding. For best results, never overload the container.

Cast-iron skillets. For even heat distribution, choose cast-iron skillets. They brown food well and can be used on top of the stove as well as in the oven. They are also very easy to clean. Choose a variety of sizes, preferably with tight-fitting lids.

Microwave oven. For today's busy cooks, "instant" cooking and reheating is essential. Cover foods with a vented, heat-proof lid to prevent messy splatters.

Hot-air corn popper. Air poppers allow you to make this crunchy treat without using any fat. To season air-popped popcorn, spray with butter-flavored nonstick spray and sprinkle lightly with butter salt or butter-flavored granules.

Food scales. It's easy to misjudge portion sizes. Use scales regularly to weigh portions and ingredients.

Slow cooker. Long, moist cooking is excellent for tough, dry cuts of meat. Slow cookers retain flavor, vitamins and minerals. Many recipes can be adapted for slow cookers, and there is no need to watch meals as they cook. Easy preparation is a great help for a cook with a busy life-style!

Steamer. Simple or elaborate, steamers easily cook foods to crisp-tender perfection without any added fat.

Freezer. With adequate freezer space, today's cook can store complete meals for quick rewarming on busy days. To speed preparation, always keep a good supply of time-savers such as grated nonfat cheeses and cooked lean meats (chicken, turkey or ham) to add to a recipe. Label each item for easy location, and wrap tightly to ensure freshness.

With the *Deliciously Healthy Favorite Foods Cookbook*, you will have the satisfaction of home-cooked meals with maximum taste and freshness and minimum fuss. You'll find that leading a low-fat life-style can be easy, as well as delicious!

Dietary Guidelines

FAT

Dietary fat has become a modern-day villain, and rightly so. In addition to making us physically overweight, excess fat in our diet also contributes to heart disease, hypertension, some cancers and diabetes. Fat contains twice as many calories as an equal weight of carbohydrates or protein. The average American diet consists of an unhealthy 40 to 50 percent fat. For weight loss, experts say that fat should only make up 15 to 20 percent of our daily calories. A low-fat diet may improve the health of those suffering from heart disease, high blood pressure, high cholesterol and diabetes. It is considered the most effective method of weight loss. Learning to recognize fatty foods is an important first step in reducing dietary fat. It is also important to recognize the different kinds of fat. Saturated fat and dietary cholesterol abound in meat, poultry, butter, cream and other dairy products made from whole milk. Substitute low-fat margarine, mayonnaise and salad dressings for high-fat products. Choose olive or canola oil, and use the least amount possible. Learn to substitute other ingredients to add flavor. Eat more vegetarian dishes, such as beans, lentils and rice.

FIBER

Most of us don't get enough fiber in our diets. Nutritionists suggest eating 20 to 30 grams of fiber a day. Rather than count grams of fiber, it's easier simply to eat several servings of fruit, vegetables, legumes and whole grains a day. Foods high in fiber are generally lower in calories and take longer to chew. Fiber allows food to pass through the digestive system more quickly. It also lowers cholesterol and helps to keep blood sugar on a more even level.

CHOLESTEROL

Cholesterol from foods such as eggs and shrimp has less impact on heart disease than does saturated fat, which causes clogged arteries and heart attacks. Reducing dietary cholesterol is less crucial than cutting back on total fat and saturated fat. Experts recommend limiting dietary cholesterol to 300 milligrams a day, a little more than the amount in one egg yolk.

PROTEIN

Protein provides essential nutrients for growth, metabolism and the repair and maintainance of our body tissues. Most American diets include too much protein. Your protein intake should supply no more than 15 to 20 percent of your total daily calories. For the leanest protein, choose skinless chicken or turkey breast, non-oily fish, seafood, meat with no marbling or fat and vegetable protein, such as beans and lentils. When planning meals, play down protein and play up other parts of the meal. Use meat as a condiment rather than as the main focus of the meal.

CARBOHYDRATES

Carbohydrates are the main source of energy for the body and the brain. They should supply 60 to 70 percent of your daily calories. Complex carbohydrates are best for a gradual release of energy. They include fresh vegetables, grains and fiber. They are great for filling you up without filling you out. Simple carbohydrates are the best source of quick energy. Fresh fruits are your healthiest choice for simple carbohydrates.

Free Foods

For persons with diabetes and for weight loss: With unlimited free foods, you will never go hungry again. You can eat unlimited quantities of the foods marked * for use anytime. Those marked **, for which portion sizes are given, may be used two or three times per day, preferably in separate servings. Carry these snacks with you so that you won't be tempted by less healthy foods. Read labels and choose foods and seasonings that are low in sodium.

VEGETABLES
Alfalfa sprouts (2 oz.)**
Cabbage (raw, 1 cup)**
Celery (raw, 1 cup)**
Cucumber (raw, 1 cup)**
Green onions (raw, 1 cup)**
Hot peppers (raw, 1 cup)**
Mushrooms (raw, 1 cup)**
Radishes (raw, 1 cup)**
Zucchini (raw, 1 cup)**

SALAD GREENS
Endive (raw, 1 cup)**
Escarole (raw, 1 cup)**
Lettuce (raw, 1 cup)**
Romaine (raw, 1 cup)**
Spinach (raw, 1 cup)**
Watercress (raw, 1 cup)**

FRUIT
Cranberries, unsweetened (½ cup)**
Rhubarb, unsweetened (½ cup)**

SWEET SUBSTITUTES (less than 20 calories per serving)
Candy, sugar-free**
Gum, sugar-free**
Jam/jelly, sugar-free (2 tsp.) **
Pancake syrup, sugar-free (1-2 tbsp.)**
Sugar substitutes (aspartame, saccharin)**
Whipped topping, "lite" (2 tbsp.)**

BEVERAGES
Bouillon, low-sodium and fat-free*
Carbonated drinks, sugar-free*
Carbonated water*
Club soda**
Cocoa powder, unsweetened (1 tbsp.)**
Coffee*
Drink mixes, sugar-free*
Tea*
Tonic water, sugar-free*

CONDIMENTS
Catsup (1 tbsp.)**
Horseradish*
Mustard*
Pickles, dill, unsweetened*
Salad dressings, low-calorie (2 tbsp.)**
Taco sauce (3 tbsp.)**

SEASONINGS
Basil*
Celery seed*
Chili powder*
Chives*
Cinnamon*
Curry powder*
Dillseed, Dillweed*
Flavoring extracts: almond, butter, lemon, mint, rum, vanilla, walnut, etc.*
Garlic, fresh*
Garlic, powdered*
Hot pepper sauce*
Lemon*
Lemon juice*
Lemon pepper*
Lime*
Lime juice*
Vinegar*
Mint*
Onion powder*
Oregano*
Paprika*
Pepper*
Pimiento*
Soy sauce, "lite"*
Wine, used in cooking (¼ cup)**
Worcestershire sauce*

Appetizers & Snacks

Quick Low-Fat Pizza	14
Buttery Popcorn	14
Curried Crab Spread	14
Sesame Shrimp Kabobs	15
Seafood Cocktail	15
Zucchini Appetizer Sticks	16
Baked Potato Skins	16
Stuffed Mushroom Caps	17
Celery Stuffed with Blue Cheese	17
Italian Chicken Salami	18
Deviled Eggs	18
Parmesan-Onion Canapés	19
Olive-Chili Quiche	19
Garbanzo Nuts	19
Low-Cal Potato Chips	20
Crispy Tortilla Chips	20
"French Fried" Onion Rings	20
Mexican Layered Dip	21
Ranch Dip	21
Chili-Cheese Dip	21
Spinach-Leek Dip	22
Spicy Salsa Dip	22
Creamy Salsa Dip	22

Quick Low-Fat Pizza

A healthy version of America's favorite snack.

1 bell pepper, cut into cubes
8 ounces mushrooms, sliced
1 prepared thin pizza crust (10 oz.)
1 cup fat-free spaghetti sauce
1½ cups grated fat-free mozzarella cheese (5 oz.)

Place pepper and mushrooms in large, heavy ovenproof skillet sprayed with nonstick spray. Oven-roast in a preheated 450° oven for 10 minutes. Meanwhile, place pizza crust on a pizza pan sprayed with nonstick spray. Spread the spaghetti sauce over the crust and scatter the grated cheese over the sauce. Bake in a preheated 450° oven for 10 minutes. Remove the roasted vegetables from the oven, and when the pizza has finished baking, scatter the roasted vegetables over the baked pizza. Serves 5.

Per serving: 187 cal. (14% from fat); 15.8 g protein; 2.9 g fat (0.82 g sat.); 25 g carbo.; 425 mg sodium; 9 mg chol.; 0.68 g fiber. Exchanges: 1 lean meat, 1 bread, 1½ vegetable.

Buttery Popcorn

Fluffy, crunchy popcorn is a dieter's best friend.

3 cups air-popped popcorn
Butter-flavored nonstick spray
Butter-flavored salt

Spray popcorn lightly with nonstick spray, then sprinkle with butter salt. Stir to mix. Serves 1.

Per serving: 117 cal. (7% from fat); 2.4 g protein; 0.9 g fat (0.15 g sat.); 13.8 g carbo.; 480 mg sodium; 0 mg chol.; 3.3 g fiber. Exchanges: 1 bread.

Curried Crab Spread

1 green onion, chopped
1 clove garlic, minced
½ teaspoon each: curry powder and Original Blend Mrs. Dash® seasoning
¼ cup fat-free mayonnaise or fat-free sour cream
1 teaspoon lemon juice
Dash Morton Lite Salt® Mixture
1 can (6 oz.) crab, drained

In a medium-size skillet sprayed with nonstick spray, stir-fry green onion and garlic over medium heat until soft. Add curry powder, Mrs. Dash®, mayonnaise or sour cream, lemon juice and Morton Lite Salt Mixture®. Cook over medium heat for 1 minute, stirring frequently. Gently stir in drained crab. Heat until warm. Serve warm with low-fat crackers or mini-toasts. Serves 6.

Per serving: 35 cal. (1% from fat); 5.8 g protein; 0.03 g fat (0.01 g sat.); 1.3 g carbo.; 161 mg sodium; 25.3 mg chol.; 0 g fiber. Exchanges: 1 lean meat. Add 1 fat exchange to meal plan.

Sesame Shrimp Kabobs

Treat your guests to an elegant appetizer.

3 tablespoons sesame seeds
1 teaspoon sesame oil
2 tablespoons lemon juice
¼ teaspoon finely grated fresh ginger
  (or use ¼ teaspoon dried ground ginger)
1 large clove garlic, minced
2 tablespoons low-sodium soy sauce
1 pound medium-large shrimp, shelled
  and deveined
4 skewers

Toast sesame seeds in a dry heavy skillet over medium heat until golden, stirring constantly. Set aside. Mix remaining ingredients. Refrigerate several hours or overnight. Remove shrimp from marinade and place on 4 skewers. Broil 3" from heat for 2 minutes, then turn and broil 3 minutes longer. Spread sesame seeds on plate. Dip each skewer into seeds to coat. Serves 4.

Per serving: 149 cal. (39% from fat); 25 g protein; 6.4 g fat (0.98 g sat.); 2.25 g carbo.; 190 mg sodium; 173 mg chol.; 0.01 g fiber. Exchanges: 3½ lean meat. Add 1 fat exchange to meal plan.

Seafood Cocktail

A low-calorie, classic favorite.

¾ cup cocktail sauce
1 tablespoon lemon juice
¼ cup minced celery
2 tablespoons minced mild onion
1 teaspoon horseradish, optional
2 drops hot pepper sauce, optional
⅓ pound cooked cocktail shrimp
⅓ pound cooked crab meat
4 lettuce leaves
4 lemon wedges

Mix cocktail sauce with lemon juice, celery, onion, horseradish (if used) and hot pepper sauce (if used). Gently stir in shrimp and crab meat. Serve on lettuce leaves with lemon wedges. Serves 4.

Per serving: 118 cal. (9% from fat); 16.6 g protein; 1.13 g fat (0.22 g sat.); 11.3 g carbo.; 552 mg sodium; 91 mg chol.; 0.1 g fiber. Exchanges: 2 lean meat, 2 vegetable. Add 1 fat exchange to meal plan.

Zucchini Appetizer Sticks

Crunchy and delicious.

2 medium zucchini, ends removed
1 egg, beaten
¼ cup fine, dry seasoned bread crumbs
¼ cup grated Parmesan cheese
½ teaspoon garlic powder
½ teaspoon Original Blend
   Mrs. Dash® seasoning

Cut zucchini into french fry-sized pieces and coat with egg. Mix crumbs, Parmesan cheese, garlic powder and Mrs. Dash® in a 9" by 13" plastic food bag. Drop a handful of zucchini pieces into crumb mixture and shake to coat. Place on 2 large cookie sheets sprayed with nonstick spray. Do not overlap pieces. Continue coating small batches of zucchini with crumb mixture until all are coated. Bake in a preheated 450° oven for 15 to 20 minutes, until coating is browned and zucchini pieces are tender. Serves 4.

Per serving: 76 cal. (37% from fat); 5.2 g protein; 3.16 g fat (1.45 g sat.); 6.8 g carbo.; 157 mg sodium; 58 mg chol.; 2.25 g fiber. Exchanges: ½ lean meat, ½ bread.

Baked Potato Skins

Easy to prepare and economical.

4 medium potatoes
   Butter-flavored nonstick spray
½ cup grated fat-free cheddar cheese
3 tablespoons very lean, cooked
   bacon bits
¼ cup minced green onion

Scrub potatoes and pierce each with a fork. Bake in a preheated 400° oven until soft— about 1 hour. Cut potatoes in half lengthwise and scoop out centers, leaving a ¼" shell. (Reserve removed potato for another use.) Cut potato halves lengthwise. Spray potato shells with butter-flavored spray, then place on a large baking sheet. Bake in a preheated 500° oven for 15 to 20 minutes, until brown and crisp. Sprinkle evenly with cheese, bacon bits and green onion. Return to 400° oven for 3 minutes longer to melt cheese. Serves 6.

Per serving: 54 cal. (5% from fat); 4.45 g protein; 0.29 g fat (0.03 g sat.); 8.8 g carbo.; 95 mg sodium; 2.67 mg chol.; 0.94 g fiber. Exchanges: ½ lean meat, ½ bread. Add ½ fat exchange to meal plan.

Stuffed Mushroom Caps

An elegant hors d'oeuvre for the most discriminating gourmet.

20 large mushrooms, rinsed
1 clove garlic, minced
⅓ cup minced onion
¼ pound ground turkey
1 egg white, beaten
3 tablespoons minced fresh parsley
2 tablespoons dry, seasoned
   bread crumbs
1½ tablespoons low-sodium soy sauce
⅛ teaspoon freshly ground pepper

Remove stems from mushrooms, mince and set aside. Place mushroom caps in a large, heavy skillet sprayed with nonstick spray. Cook for 4 minutes over medium-high heat. Turn mushrooms over and cook 3 minutes longer. Remove to a large baking sheet sprayed with nonstick spray. Respray skillet with nonstick spray and stir-fry garlic and onion over medium-high heat until soft. Remove from heat. Add turkey, egg white, minced mushroom stems, parsley, bread crumbs, soy sauce and pepper. Mix well and divide into 20 equal portions. Shape each into a ball, and press one into each mushroom cap. (If made ahead, cover and refrigerate up to overnight.) Bake stuffed mushrooms, uncovered, in a preheated 500° oven for 15 minutes. Serve hot. Serves 10.

Per serving: 42 cal. (34% from fat); 3.7 g protein; 1.6 g fat (0.41 g sat.); 2.97 g carbo.; 35 mg sodium; 9.6 mg chol.; 1.1 g fiber. Exchanges: ½ lean meat.

Celery Stuffed with Blue Cheese

Cool and crisp, with a creamy cheese stuffing.

½ cup fat-free cream cheese
1 ounce blue cheese, crumbled
½ teaspoon each: Worcestershire sauce
   and Dijon mustard
4 large stalks celery

Mix cheeses with Worcestershire sauce and mustard. Spread cheese mixture into entire length of celery stalks. Cut into 8 pieces. Serves 4.

Per serving: 57 cal. (32% from fat); 6.6 g protein; 2 g fat (1.3 g sat.); 2.55 g carbo.; 267 mg sodium; 5.3 mg chol.; 0.12 g fiber. Exchanges: 1 lean meat.

Italian Chicken Salami

Serve in thin slices.

1 pound boned, skinned chicken breast, cut into chunks
1 tablespoon grated Parmesan cheese
2 teaspoons dried, minced onion
½ teaspoon each: dried basil, marjoram and oregano
1 teaspoon Morton Lite Salt® Mixture
½ teaspoon garlic powder
   Sugar substitute equal to 1 teaspoon brown sugar (i.e., 1 teaspoon Brown SugarTwin®)

Mix all ingredients in food processor until ground. Refrigerate. Let flavors blend at least 2 hours, preferably overnight. Place mixture on piece of aluminum foil sprayed with nonstick spray. Shape meat into salami shape. Roll tightly in foil and close ends. Pierce foil all over with a fork. Set roll in baking pan. Bake in a preheated 225° oven for 3 hours. Remove foil; chill. Makes 16 servings.

Per serving: 32 cal. (12% from fat); 4.2 g protein; 0.44 g fat (0.15 g sat.); 0.01 g carbo.; 51 mg sodium; 16.2 mg chol.; 0 g fiber. Exchanges: ½ lean meat. Add ½ fat exchange to meal plan.

Deviled Eggs

Great for a picnic!

5 hard-boiled eggs, peeled and cut in half lengthwise
2 tablespoons fat-free ranch salad dressing
1 teaspoon water
½ teaspoon prepared mustard
   Dash seasoning salt
   Garnish: paprika, parsley

Remove yolks from eggs and mash. Set aside egg white halves. Mix yolks with remaining ingredients. Spoon mixture into egg white halves. Garnish tops with a dash of paprika and a small bit of parsley. Serves 5.

Per serving: 85 cal. (53% from fat); 6.2 g protein; 5 g fat (1.55 g sat.); 1 g carbo.; 107 mg sodium; 213 mg chol.; 0 g fiber. Exchanges: 1 medium-fat meat.

Parmesan-Onion Canapés

A quick-to-fix treat your guests will love.

1 cup fat-free mayonnaise
1 cup grated Parmesan cheese
½ cup thinly sliced green onion
1 French bread baguette, sliced into 24 slices (each ⅓" thick)

Mix mayonnaise, Parmesan cheese and green onion. Place the baguette slices on a large baking sheet. Broil 4" to 6" from heat until toasted on top, about 1 minute. Remove from broiler, turn. Spread 1½ tablespoons of the mayonnaise mixture on each of the baguette slices; broil until mixture is bubbly and lightly browned, 2 to 3 minutes. Serve warm. Makes 24 servings.

Per serving: 74 cal. (18% from fat); 2.4 g protein; 1.5 g fat (0.74 g sat.); 6.6 g carbo.; 200 mg sodium; 2.67 mg chol.; 0.3 g fiber. Exchanges: ½ bread.

Olive-Chili Quiche

A tasty low-fat quiche.

1 small onion, chopped
3 eggs, lightly beaten
3 egg whites, lightly beaten
8 ounces fat-free cheddar cheese, grated
¼ cup sliced black olives
¼ cup canned chili peppers, chopped
3 ounces lean ham, cut into small cubes

Stir-fry onion over medium heat in skillet sprayed with nonstick spray until golden, then cool. Mix all ingredients together. Pour into a 9" pie pan sprayed with nonstick spray. Bake in a preheated 350° oven for 30 minutes or until firm in the center. Serves 6.

Per serving: 156 cal. (38% from fat); 20.4 g protein; 6.6 g fat (1.44 g sat.); 3.5 g carbo.; 623 mg sodium; 118 mg chol.; 0.47 g fiber. Exchanges: 3 lean meat. Add ½ fat exchange to meal plan.

Garbanzo Nuts

Crunchy and satisfying!

2 cups canned garbanzo beans, drained
⅛ teaspoon butter salt or garlic salt
Butter-flavored nonstick spray

Place garbanzo beans on a large baking sheet sprayed with nonstick spray. Bake in a preheated 350° oven for 40 to 50 minutes, stirring every 5 minutes, until dry and crunchy. Spray toasted beans with butter-flavored nonstick spray and sprinkle with butter salt or garlic salt. Serves 4 (½ cup per serving).

Per serving: 50 cal. (0% from fat); 8 g protein; 0 g fat (0 g sat.); 12 g carbo.; 464 mg sodium; 0 mg chol.; 6 g fiber. Exchanges: 1 lean meat, ⅔ bread. Add ½ fat exchange to meal plan.

Low-Cal Potato Chips

Thin, crispy and delicious!

2 medium, unpeeled potatoes, sliced very thin
½ teaspoon Morton Lite Salt® Mixture

Place potato slices in a single layer on two large baking sheets sprayed with nonstick spray. Spray the slices with nonstick spray, then sprinkle with Morton Lite Salt® Mixture. Bake in a preheated 350° oven for 15 to 20 minutes, turning once. Remove chips that are golden and bake others a few minutes longer, until golden. Serves 4.

Per serving: 55 cal. (1% from fat); 1.65 g protein; 0.07 g fat (0.02 g sat.); 12.4 g carbo.; 149 mg sodium; 0 mg chol.; 1.4 g fiber. Exchanges: 1 bread.

Crispy Tortilla Chips

Serve with a low-fat dip.

4 corn tortillas
Butter-flavored nonstick spray
Butter-flavored salt, optional

Spray one side of each tortilla with nonstick spray and sprinkle lightly with butter salt (if used). Stack the tortillas and cut into 6 pie-shaped wedges. Spread the pieces out on a large baking sheet. Do not overlap pieces. Bake in a preheated 400° oven for 5 to 10 minutes, until crisp and golden. Makes 24 chips. Serves 4.

Per serving: 60 cal. (15% from fat); 1 g protein; 1 g fat (0.1 g sat.); 10 g carbo.; 170 mg sodium; 0 mg chol.; 1.7 g fiber. Exchanges: ⅔ bread.

"French Fried" Onion Rings

Serve with your favorite hot sandwich.

1 medium onion, peeled and cut into ⅓" slices
2 egg whites, lightly beaten
½ teaspoon Morton Lite Salt® Mixture
⅓ cup fine, dry bread crumbs

Separate onion slices into rings. Mix egg whites with Morton Lite Salt® Mixture. Dip each onion ring into egg white, then into the bread crumbs. Place coated rings on a large baking sheet sprayed with nonstick spray. Bake in a preheated 450° oven for 10 minutes, until crisp and golden. Serves 4.

Per serving: 51 cal. (8% from fat); 3.2 g protein; 0.44 g fat (0.13 g sat.); 8.4 g carbo.; 235 mg sodium; 0.42 mg chol.; 0.73 g fiber. Exchanges: ½ bread.

Mexican Layered Dip

Festive and easy to fix!

1 can (15 oz.) pinto beans
¼ teaspoon hot pepper sauce
1 cup grated fat-free cheddar cheese
½ cup black olives, sliced
3 green onions, sliced
1 medium tomato, chopped

Puree beans with hot pepper sauce in a blender or food processor. Pour into an 8" by 8" shallow casserole sprayed with nonstick spray. Sprinkle beans with grated cheese. Heat in a preheated 350° oven for 20 minutes (or in a microwave oven for 2 to 3 minutes), until beans are hot and cheese is melted. Scatter olives, green onions and tomato pieces over top of melted cheese. Serve with Crispy Tortilla Chips (see p. 20). Serves 12.

Per serving: 75 cal. (42% from fat); 5 g protein; 3.5 g fat (0.44 g sat.); 6.8 g carbo.; 340 mg sodium; 1.67 mg chol.; 3 g fiber. Exchanges: ½ lean meat, ½ bread, ½ fat.

Ranch Dip

Serve with a platter of raw vegetable sticks.

1 cup fat-free sour cream
1 cup low-fat (1% fat) buttermilk
1 package (1 oz.) ranch dip mix

Mix all ingredients together in a blender until smooth. Refrigerate for up to 1 week. Serves 16 (2 tablespoons per serving).

Per serving: 21 cal. (6% from fat); 1.5 g protein; 0.13 g fat (0.08 g sat.); 3.2 g carbo.; 211 mg sodium; 0.56 mg chol.; 0 g fiber. Exchanges: Free for one serving.

Chili-Cheese Dip

Serve with Crispy Tortilla Chips (see p. 20).

1 can (10¾ oz.) cream of chicken soup
1 can (4 oz.) chopped green chili peppers, drained
½ teaspoon chili powder
¾ cup grated fat-free cheddar cheese

Mix all ingredients together in a small casserole dish. Microwave until cheese is melted. Serves 12.

Per serving: 35 cal. (39% from fat); 3 g protein; 1.5 g fat (0.42 g sat.); 2.4 g carbo.; 250 mg sodium; 3.25 mg chol.; 0.08 g fiber. Exchanges: ½ lean meat.

Spinach-Leek Dip

A creamy, tangy dip. Great for parties!

1 package (1.8 oz.) leek soup mix
½ cup each: light mayonnaise and nonfat milk
1 cup fat-free sour cream
1 can (8 oz.) chopped water chestnuts
1 package (10 oz.) chopped spinach, cooked and drained

Mix all ingredients together and serve with raw vegetables. Serves 16 (3 tablespoons per serving).

Per serving: 59 cal. (48% from fat); 2.2 g protein; 3.13 g fat (0.58 g sat.); 5.7 g carbo.; 227 mg sodium; 3.56 mg chol.; 0.86 g fiber. Exchanges: 1 vegetable, ½ fat.

Spicy Salsa Dip

This is a delicious accompaniment to meats, fish and eggs.

1 cup chopped ripe tomato
¼ cup each: chopped onion and celery
1 tablespoon lemon juice
2 tablespoons chopped fresh cilantro
2 tablespoons chopped fresh or canned hot chili peppers
1 teaspoon minced garlic
Freshly ground pepper and Morton Lite Salt® Mixture, to taste, optional

Mix ingredients together. Refrigerate for several hours to let flavors blend. Serves 8 (¼ cup per serving).

Per serving: 13 cal. (12% from fat); 0.6 g protein; 0.17 g fat (0.02 g sat.); 2.9 g carbo.; 3 mg sodium; 0 mg chol.; 0.58 g fiber. Exchanges: Free for 1 serving (2 servings = 1 vegetable).

Creamy Salsa Dip

Serve with Crispy Tortilla Chips (see p. 20) or raw vegetable sticks.

½ cup fat-free sour cream or cream cheese
½ cup mild, medium or spicy salsa

Mix cream cheese and salsa together. Serves 8 (2 tablespoons per serving).

Per serving: 21 cal. (3% from fat); 2.77 g protein; 0.07 g fat (0.01 g sat.); 2.3 g carbo.; 135 mg sodium; 0 mg chol.; 0.25 g fiber. Exchanges: Free for 1 serving.

Salads & Salad Dressings

Spa Pasta Salad	24
Tomato Stuffed with Tuna Salad	24
Warm Chicken & Corn Salad	25
Chef's Salad	25
Macaroni Salad	26
Potato Salad	26
Coleslaw	26
Marinated Beet Salad	27
Zucchini Slaw	27
Cucumbers in Sour Cream	27
Marinated Bean Salad	28
Tropical Fruit Salad	28
Waldorf Salad	28
Raw Cauliflower & Apple Salad	29
Marinated Fruit Bowl	29
Pineapple-Carrot Gelatin Salad	30
Lime-Pear Gelatin Salad	30
Molded Cranberry Salad	30
Lite Italian Dressing	31
Creamy Italian Dressing	31
Ranch Dressing	31
Lite French Dressing	32
Creamy French Dressing	32
Crispy Seasoned Croutons	32

Spa Pasta Salad

A summertime treat.

¼ cup light mayonnaise
¾ cup fat-free Italian salad dressing
1½ teaspoons Original Blend
  Mrs. Dash® seasoning
10 ounces dry tricolored rotelle pasta,
  cooked according to package directions
  and drained
8 ounces cooked chicken or turkey breast,
  cut into ½" cubes
1 medium carrot, peeled and thinly sliced
¼ cup each: chopped celery and sliced
  green onion
1 cup sliced fresh mushrooms
1 cup broccoli florets or fresh edible pea
  pods (or use ½ cup of each)
  Cherry tomatoes and lettuce leaves

Mix mayonnaise with salad dressing and Mrs. Dash®. Mix gently with cooked pasta, chicken, carrot, celery, green onion, mushrooms, broccoli and/or pea pods. Serve on lettuce leaves and garnish with cherry tomatoes cut in half. Serves 6.

Per serving: 289 cal. (15% from fat); 13.4 g protein; 4.8 g fat (0.77 g sat.); 44 g carbo.; 421 mg sodium; 25 mg chol.; 3.54 g fiber. Exchanges: 1 lean meat, 3 bread.

Tomato Stuffed with Tuna Salad

A delicious light meal.

1 can (6 oz.) water-packed tuna, drained
3 tablespoons light mayonnaise
2 tablespoons each: chopped celery and
  green onion
3 medium, ripe tomatoes
3 lettuce leaves

Mix tuna, mayonnaise, celery and green onion. Core tomatoes and cut them six times from top to bottom, but do not cut completely through. Place ⅓ of the tuna salad mixture inside each tomato. Serve on a lettuce leaf. Serves 3.

Per serving: 151 cal. (40% from fat); 16.2 g protein; 6.7 g fat (1.16 g sat.); 6.3 g carbo.; 247 mg sodium; 37 mg chol.; 1.4 g fiber. Exchanges: 2 lean meat, 1 vegetable.

Warm Chicken & Corn Salad

A hearty, satisfying main course.

1 pound boneless, skinless chicken breasts, cut into bite-size pieces
2 tablespoons rice vinegar
1 teaspoon chili powder
¼ cup thinly sliced green onion
1 cup fresh, cut corn kernels (about 2 ears corn)
1 red or green bell pepper, seeded and chopped
¼ teaspoon Morton Lite Salt® Mixture
⅛ teaspoon freshly ground pepper
¼ cup minced fresh cilantro or parsley
½ pound washed spinach leaves, cut into strips
8 cherry tomatoes, cut in half

Combine chicken, vinegar, chili powder and green onion. Cover and refrigerate overnight, stirring occasionally. In a large, heavy skillet sprayed with nonstick spray, stir-fry chicken over medium-high heat until done. Remove from skillet and set aside. Respray skillet with nonstick spray. Add corn, bell pepper, Morton Lite Salt® Mixture and pepper. Stir-fry for 5 minutes. Add chicken and cilantro or parsley. Stir to mix. Serve warm chicken mixture over spinach. Garnish with cherry tomato halves. Serves 4.

Per serving: 201 cal. (10% from fat); 20 g protein; 2.34 g fat (0.53 g sat.); 17.3 g carbo.; 191 mg sodium; 65 mg chol.; 5.2 g fiber. Exchanges: 2 lean meat, 1 bread. Add ½ fat exhange to meal plan.

Chef's Salad

Serve with your favorite low-fat salad dressing.

1 cup lettuce, cut into bite-size pieces
1 small tomato, sliced or diced
2 tablespoons each: chopped celery, onion and cauliflower
1 ounce each: lean cooked chicken breast and ham, cut into julienne strips
1 ounce fat-free American cheese, cut into julienne strips
Low-fat salad dressing, optional

Place lettuce in a shallow salad bowl. Top with tomato, vegetables, cooked meats and cheese. Serves 1.

Per serving: 129 cal. (14% from fat); 20.5 g protein; 2 g fat (0.58 g sat.); 4.2 g carbo.; 551 mg sodium; 30 mg chol.; 1.7 g fiber. Exchanges: 2½ lean meat, 1 vegetable. Add 1 fat exchange to meal plan.

Macaroni Salad

Satisfying enough to be a main dish.

6 ounces dry elbow macaroni, cooked according to package directions and drained
3 ounces lean ham, cut into small cubes
3 ounces fat-free American cheese, cut into small cubes
2 tablespoons minced green onions
3 tablespoons each: bell pepper and fresh parsley, chopped
¼ cup chopped celery
½ cup fat-free ranch salad dressing

In a mixing bowl, combine all ingredients; refrigerate for several hours before serving so that flavors can blend. Serves 5.

Per serving: 187 cal. (7% from fat); 13.7 g protein; 1.43 g fat (0.37 g sat.); 28 g carbo.; 524 mg sodium; 8.3 mg chol.; 1.36 g fiber. Exchanges: 1 lean meat, 1½ bread, 1 vegetable.

Potato Salad

A family favorite!

½ cup light mayonnaise
¼ cup each: minced dill pickles and pickle juice
1 teaspoon Original Blend Mrs. Dash® seasoning
4 cups (2 lbs.) cooked, peeled and cubed potatoes
2 hard-boiled eggs, chopped
½ cup chopped celery
2 green onions, minced

In a large mixing bowl, combine mayonnaise, pickles, pickle juice and Mrs. Dash®. Add potatoes, eggs, celery and green onions. Stir to mix. Refrigerate for several hours before serving to let flavors blend. Serves 10.

Per serving: 114 cal. (40% from fat); 2.47 g protein; 5.1 g fat (0.93 g sat.); 14.7 g carbo.; 185 mg sodium; 47 mg chol.; 0.32 g fiber. Exchanges: 1 bread, 1 fat.

Coleslaw

½ small green cabbage, grated
1 medium carrot, peeled and grated
¼ cup light mayonnaise
1 tablespoon rice vinegar
Sugar substitute equal to 2 teaspoons sugar (i.e., 1 packet Equal®)

In a mixing bowl, combine all ingredients. Refrigerate. Let flavors blend for at least one hour before serving. Serves 5.

Per serving: 44 cal. (46% from fat); 0.95 g protein; 2.23 g fat (0.33 g sat.); 5.8 g carbo.; 67 mg sodium; 2 mg chol.; 0.77 g fiber. Exchanges: 1 vegetable, ½ fat.

Marinated Beet Salad

Beets in a light, tangy dressing.

2 cups cooked, sliced beets (drained, if canned)
½ cup fat-free Italian salad dressing
½ teaspoon Original Blend Mrs. Dash® seasoning
2 tablespoons sliced green onion

In a mixing bowl, combine all ingredients. Refrigerate for several hours before serving to let flavors blend. Serves 5.

Per serving: 36 cal. (2% from fat); 0.75 g protein; 0.06 g fat (0.01 g sat.); 7.7 g carbo.; 510 mg sodium; 0 mg chol.; 1.68 g fiber. Exchanges: 1 vegetable.

Zucchini Slaw

Colorful and delicious!

2 medium zucchini, with ends removed, coarsely grated
1 green onion, thinly sliced
¼ cup chopped celery
½ cup chopped red bell pepper
⅓ cup fat-free Italian salad dressing
2 cloves garlic, finely minced
2 teaspoons olive oil
1 teaspoon Original Blend Mrs. Dash® seasoning

In a mixing bowl, combine all ingredients. Chill for at least one hour to let flavors blend. Serves 6.

Per serving: 27 cal. (55% from fat); 0.58 g protein; 1.65 g fat (0.22 g sat.); 3.27 g carbo.; 151 mg sodium; 0 mg chol.; 1.5 g fiber. Exchanges: ½ vegetable.

Cucumbers in Sour Cream

Cucumber slices in a rich-tasting, slightly spicy dressing.

1 cucumber, peeled and thinly sliced
½ teaspoon Morton Lite Salt® Mixture
⅓ cup fat-free sour cream
2 tablespoons minced chives or green onion
1 drop hot pepper sauce
¼ teaspoon dried dillweed
2 tablespoons rice vinegar
Freshly ground pepper to taste

In a nonmetallic bowl, mix cucumber slices with Morton Lite Salt® Mixture. Mix remaining ingredients in a large measuring cup. After ½ hour, drain the cucumbers well and stir in sour cream mixture. Chill for ½ hour before serving. Serves 5.

Per serving: 18 cal. (4% from fat); 1.27 g protein; 0.08 g fat (0.02 g sat.); 3.2 g carbo.; 68 mg sodium; 0 mg chol.; 0.38 g fiber. Exchanges: Free for 1 serving.

Marinated Bean Salad

Hearty and satisfying!

1 can (15 oz.) each: kidney, cut green and garbanzo beans, drained
1 can (15 oz.) plain artichoke hearts, drained
¾ cup fat-free Italian salad dressing
2 tablespoons olive oil, optional
¼ cup each: minced celery and green onion
1 teaspoon finely minced garlic

In a large mixing bowl, combine all ingredients. Refrigerate for several hours before serving to let flavors blend. Serves 10.

Per serving: 103 cal. (6% from fat); 5 g protein; 0.65 g fat (0.08 g sat.); 19.8 g carbo.; 445 mg sodium; 0 mg chol.; 4.6 g fiber. Exchanges: 1 bread, 1 vegetable.

Tropical Fruit Salad

A refreshing blend of tropical flavors.

1 ripe papaya or mango, peeled, seeded and cubed
1 banana, sliced
1 cup juice-pack pineapple chunks with juice
2 tablespoons shredded dried coconut
4 mint sprigs

In a mixing bowl, combine all ingredients except mint. Garnish each serving with a sprig of mint. Serves 4.

Per serving: 108 cal. (11% from fat); 1.1 g protein; 1.33 g fat (0.99 g sat.); 25.3 g carbo.; 10.9 mg sodium; 0 mg chol.; 1.87 g fiber. Exchanges: 1½ fruit.

Waldorf Salad

An old-fashioned favorite.

3 tablespoons light mayonnaise
1 tablespoon each: lemon juice and water
  Sugar substitute equal to 2 teaspoons sugar (i.e., 1 packet Equal®)
2 medium apples, cored and diced
2 stalks celery, diced
4 small lettuce leaves
2 tablespoons chopped walnuts

In a mixing bowl, combine mayonnaise with lemon juice, water and sugar substitute. Add apples and celery. Stir to mix. Spoon onto lettuce leaves and sprinkle with walnuts. Serves 4.

Per serving: 107 cal. (53% from fat); 1.35 g protein; 6.3 g fat (0.76 g sat.); 12.8 g carbo.; 106 mg sodium; 3.75 mg chol.; 2.4 g fiber. Exchanges: 1 fruit, 1 fat.

Raw Cauliflower & Apple Salad

Crunchy and flavorful!

3 unpeeled red apples, cored and diced
1 small head cauliflower, thinly sliced
1 cup sliced celery
2 green onions, sliced
½ cup chopped fresh parsley
1 clove garlic, minced
¾ cup fat-free Italian salad dressing
1 tablespoon olive oil, optional
8 small lettuce leaves

Place apples, cauliflower, celery, green onions and parsley in a large mixing bowl. Mix garlic with salad dressing and olive oil (if used). Pour over apple mixture and stir to mix. Serve on lettuce leaves. Serves 8.

Per serving: 62 cal. (5% from fat); 1.97 g protein; 0.37 g fat (0.07 g sat.); 15 g carbo.; 244 mg sodium; 0 mg chol.; 2.45 g fiber. Exchanges: 1 vegetable, ⅔ fruit.

Marinated Fruit Bowl

A colorful mixture of fresh fruit.

2 cups fresh strawberries, cut in half
1 cup seedless grapes
1 cup honeydew melon or cantaloupe, cut into cubes or balls
2 kiwifruits, peeled and sliced ¼" thick
1 cup Red Delicious apple, cut into ½" cubes
1 banana, sliced
1 tablespoon lime or lemon juice
Sugar substitute equal to 4 teaspoons sugar (i.e., 2 packets Equal®)

Place all fruit in a mixing bowl. Mix lime or lemon juice with sugar substitute and add to fruit. Stir gently to mix. Serves 8.

Per serving: 69 cal. (6% from fat); 1.08 g protein; 0.44 g fat (0.07 g sat.); 17 g carbo.; 7.9 mg sodium; 0 mg chol.; 2.74 g fiber. Exchanges: 1 fruit.

Pineapple-Carrot Gelatin Salad

A refreshing, "lite" salad.

1 package (0.6 oz.) orange-flavored sugar-free gelatin mix
2 cups boiling water
1½ cups cool water
1 cup juice-pack crushed pineapple
1 cup finely grated carrot

Dissolve gelatin in boiling water. Let cool for 10 minutes. Add cool water, pineapple and grated carrot. Refrigerate until it begins to thicken. Stir well, then pour into 1 large mold or 8 individual molds. Refrigerate until set, about 1 hour. Serves 8.

Per serving: 33 cal. (1% from fat); 1.26 g protein; 0.05 g fat (0.01 g sat.); 6.3 g carbo.; 55 mg sodium; 0 mg chol.; 0.39 g fiber. Exchanges: ½ bread.

Lime-Pear Gelatin Salad

1 can (16 oz.) juice-pack pear halves
1 package (0.6 oz.) lime-flavored sugar-free gelatin mix
2 cups boiling water
8 ounces vanilla-flavored nonfat yogurt

Drain pears, then cut into ½" slices. Reserve 1 cup juice. Dissolve gelatin in boiling water, then let cool for 10 minutes. Measure 1 cup gelatin mixture; blend in yogurt and pour into 8" square pan. Chill until set but not firm. Add measured pear juice to remaining gelatin and chill until slightly thickened. Arrange pear slices on gelatin-yogurt layer. Top with gelatin-pear juice mixture and chill until firm, about 3 hours. To serve, cut into squares. Serves 8.

Per serving: 53 cal. (0% from fat); 2.6 g protein; 0.04 g fat (0 g sat.); 10 g carbo.; 75 mg sodium; 0 mg chol.; 1 g fiber. Exchanges: ⅔ fruit.

Molded Cranberry Salad

A delicious accompaniment to turkey.

1 package (0.6 oz.) strawberry-flavored sugar-free gelatin mix
2 cups boiling water
2 cups cold water
1 cup raw cranberries, chopped or coarsely ground
1 apple, cored and diced
½ cup chopped celery
Lettuce leaves

Dissolve gelatin in boiling water. Add cold water and let cool in refrigerator, until it begins to thicken. Stir in cranberries, apple and celery. Pour into one large mold or 8 individual molds. When firm, serve on lettuce leaves. Serves 8.

Per serving: 25 cal. (4% from fat); 1.13 g protein; 0.1 g fat (0.02 g sat.); 4.4 g carbo.; 57 mg sodium; 0 mg chol.; 1.46 g fiber. Exchanges: ⅓ fruit.

Lite Italian Dressing

Perfect for salads or marinades.

⅔ cup water
2 teaspoons arrowroot or cornstarch
3 tablespoons rice vinegar or red wine vinegar
1 tablespoon each: lemon juice and olive oil
1 small clove garlic, minced
⅛ teaspoon each: freshly ground pepper and crushed dried oregano leaves
1 teaspoon each: Original Blend Mrs. Dash® seasoning and Dijon mustard
½ teaspoon Morton Lite Salt® Mixture
Sugar substitute equal to 2 teaspoons sugar (i.e., 1 packet Equal®)

In a small saucepan, blend water and arrowroot or cornstarch. Bring to a boil, stirring constantly. Remove from heat immediately and chill by setting pan in ice water. Mix in remaining ingredients and chill well before serving. Refrigerate for up to 2 weeks. Serves 8 (2 tablespoons per serving).

Per serving: 20 cal. (81% from fat); 0.03 g protein; 1.8 g fat (0.24 g sat.); 1.15 g carbo.; 80 mg sodium; 0 mg chol.; 0 g fiber. Exchanges: Free for 1 serving.

Creamy Italian Dressing

A light, tangy flavor.

1 cup fat-free Italian salad dressing
½ cup light mayonnaise
½ cup water

Mix all ingredients together in a blender until smooth. Refrigerate for up to 2 weeks. Serves 15 (2 tablespoons per serving).

Per serving: 32 cal. (75% from fat); 0 g protein; 2.67 g fat (0.4 g sat.); 2.13 g carbo.; 216 mg sodium; 2.67 mg chol.; 0 g fiber. Exchanges: ½ fat.

Ranch Dressing

Creamy and rich-tasting.

¼ cup light mayonnaise
¼ cup fat-free mayonnaise
1½ cups low-fat (1% fat) buttermilk
½ teaspoon each: garlic salt, onion salt and Original Blend Mrs. Dash® seasoning
1 teaspoon dried parsley flakes

Mix all ingredients together in a blender until smooth. Refrigerate for up to 2 weeks. Serves 8 (2 tablespoons per serving).

Per serving: 62 cal. (42% from fat); 1.52 g protein; 2.9 g fat (0.63 g sat.); 2.76 g carbo.; 354 mg sodium; 4.2 mg chol.; 0 g fiber. Exchanges: ½ vegetable, ½ fat.

Lite French Dressing

A classic, low-fat dressing.

⅔ cup tomato-vegetable juice
2 teaspoons arrowroot or cornstarch
2 tablespoons rice vinegar
1 teaspoon Dijon mustard
½ teaspoon Original Blend Mrs. Dash® seasoning
2 teaspoons olive oil
1 small clove garlic, minced

In a small saucepan blend juice with arrowroot or cornstarch. Bring to a boil, stirring constantly. Remove from heat immediately and chill by setting pan in ice water. Add vinegar, mustard, Mrs. Dash®, oil and garlic. Chill well before serving. Refrigerate for up to 1 week. Serves 7 (2 tablespoons per serving).

Per serving: 20 cal. (63% from fat); 0.17 g protein; 1.4 g fat (0.18 g sat.); 2.1 g carbo.; 93 mg sodium; 0 mg chol.; 0.28 g fiber. Exchanges: Free for 1 serving.

Creamy French Dressing

Low in fat, yet rich in flavor.

⅔ cup tomato-vegetable juice
2 tablespoons rice vinegar
1 teaspoon Dijon mustard
½ teaspoon Original Blend Mrs. Dash® seasoning
1 small clove garlic, minced
¼ cup light mayonnaise

Mix all ingredients in a blender until smooth. Chill well before serving. Refrigerate for up to 1 week. Serves 10 (2 tablespoons per serving).

Per serving: 26 cal. (71% from fat); 0.12 g protein; 2.04 g fat (0.3 g sat.); 1.88 g carbo.; 111 mg sodium; 2 mg chol.; 0.2 g fiber. Exchanges: ½ fat.

Crispy Seasoned Croutons

Add crunch to your salads.

4 slices French bread
½ teaspoon garlic powder
1 teaspoon Original Blend Mrs. Dash® seasoning

Spray bread slices on both sides with butter-flavored nonstick spray. Sprinkle both sides with garlic powder and Mrs. Dash®. Stack the slices of seasoned bread and cut into ½" cubes. Place on a baking sheet and toast in a preheated 350° oven, stirring frequently, until golden—about 10 to 15 minutes. Serves 8.

Per serving: 35 cal. (13% from fat); 1 g protein; 0.5 g fat (0.1 g sat.); 6.5 g carbo.; 73 mg sodium; 0 mg chol.; 0.3 g fiber. Exchanges: ½ bread.

Soups & Chowders

Beef-Vegetable Soup

Great for a chilly day, and so nutritious!

1 beef shank bone with 1 lb. meat
2½ quarts water
2 bay leaves
⅓ cup chopped celery leaves
¼ cup chopped fresh parsley
1 teaspoon Morton Lite Salt® Mixture
½ teaspoon freshly ground pepper
1 envelope (1 oz.) onion soup mix
1 can (15 oz.) stewed tomatoes with juice
1 package (10 oz.) frozen
   mixed vegetables
1 cup peeled, diced potatoes
1 cup sliced celery

Remove any fat from beef. In a large, covered soup pot, simmer the beef bone with meat in water with bay leaves, celery leaves, parsley, Morton Lite Salt® Mixture, pepper and onion soup mix until meat is tender, about 2½ hours. Remove the bone, meat and bay leaves. Chill broth and remove any fat. Cut meat into bite-size pieces and return to broth. Discard bone and bay leaves. Add tomatoes, frozen vegetables, potatoes and celery. Cover and simmer for 25 minutes. Serves 10.

Per serving: 106 cal. (21% from fat); 12.2 g protein; 2.46 g fat (0.8 g sat.); 8.6 g carbo.; 306 mg sodium; 28 mg chol.; 2.1 g fiber. Exchanges: 1 lean meat, ½ bread, 1 vegetable.

New England-Style Clam Chowder

Creamy, rich-tasting and delicious.

1 medium onion, chopped
1 cup water
2 medium potatoes, peeled and cut into
   ½" cubes (about 2 cups)
2 cans (6 oz. each) chopped or minced
   clams (use clam juice)
3 packages (1 teaspoon each) chicken
   bouillon granules
4 cups low-fat (1% fat) milk
3 tablespoons each: flour and cornstarch,
   mixed with ½ cup water in a blender
   Freshly ground pepper to taste
¼ cup very lean, cooked bacon bits

In a large, heavy soup pot sprayed with nonstick spray, stir-fry onion over medium heat until soft. Add water, potatoes, clams and chicken bouillon granules. Simmer until potatoes are tender, about 10 minutes. Add milk, flour-cornstarch mixture and pepper. Cook over medium heat, stirring constantly, until thickened. Ladle into 6 large soup bowls and garnish with bacon bits. Serves 6.

Per serving: 177 cal. (13% from fat); 12.8 g protein; 2.46 g fat (1.14 g sat.); 24 g carbo.; 883 mg sodium; 23 mg chol.; 0.54 g fiber. Exchanges: ½ lean meat, 1 bread, ¾ nonfat milk.

Ham & Bean Soup

This soup is hearty and full of flavor.

1 cup sliced green onion
1 cup diced celery
1 large clove garlic, minced
½ teaspoon dried thyme leaves
4 cups low-sodium chicken broth
3 cups water
1 can (15 oz.) cooked cannellini beans (white kidney beans) or navy beans
2 ounces uncooked elbow macaroni
½ pound lean ham, diced
⅛ teaspoon freshly ground pepper
¼ cup chopped fresh parsley
2-3 drops hot red pepper sauce

In a large saucepan sprayed with nonstick spray, stir-fry green onion, celery, garlic and thyme over medium-high heat for 2 to 3 minutes, until tender. Add broth and water. Bring to a boil. Meanwhile, puree half the beans at a time in a blender or food processor. Add macaroni, ham, pepper, parsley, hot pepper sauce and beans to boiling soup stock. Simmer, covered, for 30 minutes. Serves 8.

Per serving: 165 cal. (16% from fat); 16.2 g protein; 2.94 g fat (0.9 g sat.); 18 g carbo.; 562 mg sodium; 9.4 mg chol.; 5.2 g fiber. Exchanges: 2 lean meat, 1 bread. Add ½ fat exchange to meal plan.

Leek-Mushroom Soup

A gourmet dish that is sure to please.

6 large leeks
½ pound mushrooms, sliced
2 cloves garlic, minced
½ teaspoon dried tarragon leaves
¼ teaspoon white pepper
⅓ cup flour
2 cups low-fat (1% fat) milk
4 cups low-sodium chicken broth

Trim root ends and tough, dark green tops off leeks. Split leeks lengthwise, rinse with water, and slice thinly to make 1 quart of cut leeks. In a large, heavy soup pot sprayed with nonstick spray, cook leeks, mushrooms, garlic, tarragon and pepper over medium-high heat, stirring often, for 15 minutes. Cover pot if vegetables become too dry. In a blender, mix flour with milk. Add to cooked vegetables. Add chicken broth and cook over medium heat, stirring constantly, until thickened. Serves 8.

Per serving: 115 cal. (16% from fat); 8.7 g protein; 2.1 g fat (0.8 g sat.); 15.7 g carbo.; 407 mg sodium; 3.6 mg chol.; 1.38 g fiber. Exchanges: 2 vegetable, ½ low-fat milk.

French Onion Soup

A classic favorite without the fat.

2 medium onions, thinly sliced
⅛ teaspoon coarsely ground pepper
1 tablespoon flour
4 cups low-sodium beef broth
1 bay leaf
4 slices French bread
2 tablespoons grated Parmesan cheese

In a large, heavy saucepan sprayed with nonstick spray, stir-fry onions over medium-high heat until onions are a light golden brown. Cover pan if onions get too dry. Sprinkle onions with pepper and flour; stir well. Cook 1 minute longer, stirring constantly. Add beef broth and bay leaf. Cover and simmer for 30 minutes. Discard bay leaf. Toast the bread until golden brown. Sprinkle toast evenly with Parmesan cheese, then microwave until cheese is melted. Pour soup into 4 bowls. Place one piece of cheese toast on top of each serving of soup. Serves 4.

Per serving: 123 cal. (17% from fat); 6.7 g protein; 2.3 g fat (0.95 g sat.); 19 g carbo.; 251 mg sodium; 2 mg chol.; 1.45 g fiber. Exchanges: 1 bread, 1 vegetable, ½ fat.

Turkey-Vegetable Soup

Garden-fresh flavor, and a meal in itself!

1 pound ground turkey or chicken breast
½ teaspoon dried thyme leaves
2 tablespoons sliced green onion
2 tablespoons cornstarch
½ teaspoon garlic salt
¼ teaspoon pepper
8 cups low-sodium chicken broth
6 medium carrots, peeled and sliced
3 stalks celery, sliced
2 medium zucchini, cut into ¼" slices
2 cups uncooked medium-wide egg noodles or rotelle pasta
¼ cup chopped fresh parsley

Mix turkey, thyme, green onion, cornstarch, garlic salt and pepper. Shape into 1" meatballs. Place chicken broth in a large soup pot and bring to a boil. Add carrots and celery. Simmer for 5 minutes. Add meatballs, zucchini, noodles or pasta and parsley to simmering chicken broth. Simmer for 15 minutes longer. Serves 8.

Per serving: 217 cal. (14% from fat); 26.5 g protein; 3.4 g fat (0.96 g sat.); 19 g carbo.; 238 mg sodium; 37.4 mg chol.; 2.04 g fiber. Exchanges: 2 lean meat, 1½ bread, 1 vegetable. Add ½ fat exchange to meal plan.

Goulash Soup

A hearty soup with old-world flavor.

1 cup chopped onion
1 clove garlic, minced
½ pound lean round steak, cut into ½" cubes
4 cups water
1 beef bouillon cube
1-2 tablespoons paprika
½ teaspoon Morton Lite Salt® Mixture
2 ounces tomato paste (or substitute 1 peeled tomato, cut up)
1 medium potato, peeled and diced

In a large, heavy soup pot sprayed with nonstick spray, stir-fry onion and garlic until golden brown. Remove from pot and set aside. Respray pot with nonstick spray and brown beef cubes over medium-high heat. Add cooked onion and garlic to pot. Add water, bouillon cube, paprika, Morton Lite Salt® Mixture and tomato paste or tomato. Cover and simmer for 4 hours. Add potato and simmer for 15 minutes longer. Serves 6.

Per serving: 91 cal. (20% from fat); 10 g protein; 2 g fat (0.68 g sat.); 8.1 g carbo.; 290 mg sodium; 23.4 mg chol.; 0.62 g fiber. Exchanges: 1 lean meat, ½ bread.

Chili-Bean Soup

Make a day ahead so that flavors can blend and mellow.

⅓ cup chopped green bell pepper
1 small onion, chopped
⅓ pound lean round steak, sliced into very thin 1" long strips
4 cups low-sodium beef bouillon
1½ teaspoons each: chili powder and dried parsley flakes
3 cups canned peeled tomatoes (with juice), cut into pieces
3 tablespoons cornstarch, dissolved in ½ cup water
1 can (15 oz.) pink or pinto beans with juice

In a large, heavy soup pot sprayed with nonstick spray, stir-fry pepper and onion over medium-high heat until soft but not browned. Remove from pot and set aside. Respray pot with nonstick spray and brown beef strips over medium-high heat. Add cooked pepper and onion to pot. Add beef bouillon, chili powder, parsley, tomatoes with juice, cornstarch dissolved in water and beans with juice. Cover and simmer for 1 hour. Serves 8.

Per serving: 101 cal. (26% from fat); 7.1 g protein; 2.9 g fat (1.1 g sat.); 12.3 g carbo.; 395 mg sodium; 9 mg chol.; 4.8 g fiber. Exchanges: 1 lean meat, 1 bread.

Bouillabaisse

Serve with crusty French bread and a green salad.

1 small carrot, peeled and chopped
¼ cup finely chopped celery
½ cup finely chopped onion
1 clove garlic, minced
1½ cups peeled and cubed tomatoes
⅛ teaspoon crumbled saffron threads, optional
¼ teaspoon dried oregano leaves
2 cups water
1 small bay leaf
1½ teaspoons chicken bouillon granules
1 tablespoon chopped fresh parsley
Freshly ground pepper to taste
1 teaspoon lemon juice
½ cup white wine (or substitute ½ cup chicken broth)
1 tablespoon cornstarch, mixed with 3 tablespoons water
½ pound boneless fish filets
½ pound medium, raw shrimp, shelled
6 small clams in the shell, washed

In a large, heavy saucepan sprayed with nonstick spray, stir-fry carrot, celery, onion and garlic over medium heat until tender. Add tomatoes, saffron (if used), oregano, water, bay leaf, chicken bouillon granules, parsley, pepper, lemon juice and wine (or chicken broth). Simmer for 10 minutes. Stir in cornstarch mixed with water, fish filets, shrimp and clams. Cover and simmer for 5 to 10 minutes longer. Discard bay leaf. Serves 3.

Per serving: 232 cal. (11% from fat); 34.5 g protein; 2.83 g fat (0.53 g sat.); 13 g carbo.; 785 mg sodium; 165 mg chol.; 1.52 g fiber. Exchanges: 4 lean meat, 2 vegetable. Add 2 fat exchanges to meal plan.

Chilled Gazpacho

A refreshing addition to a summer meal.

3 very ripe, medium tomatoes, cored, peeled and chopped
1 medium cucumber, peeled and chopped
1 green bell pepper, seeded and minced
½ cup chopped red onion
1 cup tomato juice
1 clove garlic, minced
2 tablespoons lemon juice or wine vinegar
1 tablespoon olive oil, optional
½ teaspoon Morton Lite Salt® Mixture
¼ teaspoon freshly ground pepper
3 drops hot pepper sauce, optional

Mix all ingredients together. Refrigerate until chilled, at least 1 hour. Serve cold. Serves 4.

Per serving: 49 cal. (4% from fat); 2 g protein; 0.44 g fat (0.07 g sat.); 10.9 g carbo.; 276 mg sodium; 0 mg chol.; 2.55 g fiber. Exchanges: ⅔ bread or 2 vegetable.

Creamy Potato Soup

Creamy, rich flavor, yet low in fat.

1 medium onion, diced
7 cups water, divided
4 medium (1½ lbs.) potatoes, peeled and sliced
1 bay leaf
1½ cups lightly packed coarsely grated or chopped cabbage
1 cup coarsely grated carrot
½ cup thinly sliced celery
¼ cup chopped fresh parsley
1 teaspoon dried basil
½ teaspoon freshly ground pepper
3 packages (1 teaspoon each) chicken bouillon granules
1 envelope low-fat (½% fat) milk powder (equal to 1 quart milk)
2 tablespoons flour

In a large, heavy saucepan sprayed with nonstick spray, brown onion over medium heat. Remove onion. Add 3 cups water, potatoes and bay leaf. Cover and simmer until potatoes are tender—about 10 minutes. Discard bay leaf. Remove potatoes with a slotted spoon to blender or food processor. Add 2 cups water and puree. Return pureed potatoes (with liquid) and onions to saucepan. Add cabbage, carrot, celery, parsley, basil, pepper and chicken bouillon granules. Simmer 10 minutes. Mix milk powder, 2 cups water and flour in blender. Add to soup, stirring often. Cook over medium heat until thickened. Serves 6.

Per serving: 149 cal. (10% from fat); 8.2 g protein; 1.6 g fat (0.8 g sat.); 26.4 g carbo.; 665 mg sodium; 5.2 mg chol.; 1 g fiber. Exchanges: 1 bread, ¾ nonfat milk.

Swiss Soup

Very low in calories, but a satisfying snack or meal accompaniment.

¼ cup chopped green onion
½ cup chopped celery
1 large carrot, peeled and chopped
¼ cup chopped green bell pepper
6 cups low-sodium chicken broth
2 cups coarsely grated or chopped cabbage
Dash freshly ground pepper

In a large soup pot sprayed with nonstick spray, stir-fry onion and celery over medium-high heat until soft but not browned. Add remaining ingredients and simmer, covered, for 20 minutes. Serves 7.

Per serving: 26 cal. (18% from fat); 2.8 g protein; 0.51 g fat (0.24 g sat.); 2.94 g carbo.; 114 mg sodium; 0 mg chol.; 0.45 g fiber. Exchanges: 1 vegetable.

Quick Minestrone

Hearty vegetable flavor!

¼ pound lean ham, cut into small pieces
1 can (10¾ oz.) condensed onion soup
2 cups canned tomatoes (with juice), cut into pieces
½ cup each: diced carrot and celery
1 medium zucchini, diced
1 large clove garlic, minced
⅓ cup minced fresh parsley
1 bay leaf
¼ teaspoon each: dried thyme leaves, marjoram, basil and pepper
5 cups water
1 cup broken uncooked spaghetti
1 can (15 oz.) cannellini, navy or other white beans, undrained
¼ cup grated Parmesan cheese

In a large soup pot, combine ham, soup, tomatoes, carrot, celery, zucchini, garlic, parsley, bay leaf, thyme, marjoram, basil, pepper and water. Simmer, covered, for 1 hour. Add spaghetti and beans with liquid and cook 30 minutes longer. Remove bay leaf. Sprinkle each serving with Parmesan cheese. Serves 8.

Per serving: 122 cal. (18% from fat); 8.9 g protein; 2.4 g fat (0.86 g sat.); 17.2 g carbo.; 871 mg sodium; 6.1 mg chol.; 5.3 g fiber. Exchanges: 1 lean meat, 1 bread.

Hearty Mushroom-Barley Soup

Chicken broth gives this soup a rich flavor.

2 cups each: low-sodium chicken broth and water
½ cup barley
2 carrots, peeled and diced
2 stalks celery, diced
1 onion, chopped
½ pound mushrooms, thickly sliced
⅛ teaspoon pepper
5 ounces frozen peas
8 ounces cooked chicken breast, cubed
1 can (10¾ oz.) condensed cream of chicken soup
½ cup nonfat milk

In a covered pan, simmer chicken broth, water and barley for 30 minutes. Add carrots, celery, onion, mushrooms and pepper. Simmer, covered, for 10 minutes. Add peas, chicken, soup and milk. Simmer 5 minutes longer. Serves 6.

Per serving: 195 cal. (24% from fat); 11.1 g protein; 5.2 g fat (1.38 g sat.); 23 g carbo.; 385 mg sodium; 24 mg chol.; 3.1 g fiber. Exchanges: 1 lean meat, 1½ bread.

Beef, Veal, Pork & Lamb

Roast Filet Mignon with Mushrooms

An elegant dinner entrée.

1½ pounds lean, whole filet mignon, trimmed of fat
2 cloves garlic, cut into slivers
1 teaspoon Original Blend Mrs. Dash® seasoning, divided
3 cups sliced mushrooms
½ cup sliced green onion
½ teaspoon Morton Lite Salt® Mixture

Make small cuts in filet and insert garlic slivers. Sprinkle ½ teaspoon Mrs. Dash® over meat. Place filet in a large, heavy ovenproof skillet sprayed with nonstick spray. Roast in a preheated 450° oven. Cook 15 to 20 minutes for rare, 25 to 30 minutes for medium, or 35 to 40 minutes for well done. Remove roast from oven and let stand for 10 minutes on a warm serving platter. Meanwhile, add mushrooms and green onion to skillet. Sprinkle with Morton Lite Salt® Mixture and ½ teaspoon Mrs. Dash®. Roast vegetables for 10 minutes. Slice meat and serve with cooked mushrooms and green onion. Serves 6.

Per serving: 178 cal. (43% from fat); 24 g protein; 8.4 g fat (3 g sat.); 1.8 g carbo.; 145 mg sodium; 70 mg chol.; 0.9 g fiber. Exchanges: 3½ lean meat.

Quick Beef Stroganoff

Serve with plain rice or noodles.

1 pound lean round steak, cut diagonally across the grain into thin strips
2 tablespoons flour
1½ cups water
⅓ envelope (1 oz.) onion soup mix
1 can (6 oz.) sliced mushrooms with juice
¾ cup fat-free sour cream

In a large, heavy skillet sprayed with nonstick spray, brown beef strips over high heat, stirring constantly. Reduce heat. Mix flour with water. Add to beef in skillet. Add onion soup mix and mushrooms with juice. Stir to mix. Cover and simmer until beef is tender—about 1 hour. Stir in sour cream and heat, but do not boil. Serves 4.

Per serving: 212 cal. (23% from fat); 27.5 g protein; 5.5 g fat (1.87 g sat.); 9.6 g carbo.; 269 mg sodium; 68 mg chol.; 0.59 g fiber. Exchanges: 4 lean meat, ½ bread. Add 1 fat exchange to meal plan.

Easy Beef Stew

A hearty family favorite.

2 pounds very lean stew meat, cut into large cubes
1 pound carrots, peeled and cut into large chunks
4 medium potatoes, peeled and cut into large pieces
16 medium boiling onions, peeled
2 stalks celery, cut into 1" slices
1 envelope (1 oz.) onion soup mix
1 can (10¾ oz.) condensed cream of mushroom soup

Remove any fat from meat. Combine all ingredients in a Crockpot. Cook on low for 10 to 12 hours or on high for 5 to 6 hours. (Note: stew can be baked in a tightly covered casserole dish at 250° for 5 to 6 hours. Add 1 cup water if baking stew.) Serves 8.

Per serving: 278 cal. (27% from fat); 29 g protein; 8.4 g fat (2.7 g sat.); 21 g carbo.; 463 mg sodium; 70 mg chol.; 1.27 g fiber. Exchanges: 3 lean meat, 1 bread, 1 vegetable.

Carrot Meatloaf

Simple to prepare and sure to please.

1 pound very lean ground beef
½ pound low-fat turkey sausage
½ cup uncooked oats, quick or old-fashioned
2 eggs, beaten
⅓ cup finely chopped onion
¾ cup fresh bread crumbs (grind fresh bread in a blender or food processor)
1½ cups grated carrot
⅔ cup chopped green bell pepper
½ can (8 oz.) tomato sauce
1 teaspoon seasoning salt
½ teaspoon Morton Lite Salt® Mixture
¼ teaspoon pepper

Mix all ingredients together. Shape into a loaf and bake in a preheated 350° oven for 1 hour and 10 minutes. Serves 7.

Per serving: 264 cal. (46% from fat); 20 g protein; 13.5 g fat (4.8 g sat.); 15 g carbo.; 378 mg sodium; 120 mg chol.; 0.9 g fiber. Exchanges: 2½ lean meat, 1 bread.

Sirloin Tips in Mushroom-Wine Sauce

The wine and mushrooms add a piquant flavor.

1½ pounds lean sirloin tips, cut into
    6 serving-size pieces
1 cup beef bouillon
½ cup dry white or red wine (dry
    vermouth is especially good)
1 large clove garlic, minced
1 teaspoon Italian seasoning
2 cups sliced mushrooms
2 tablespoons flour
¼ cup water

In a large, heavy skillet sprayed with nonstick spray, brown sirloin tips over medium-high heat. Add bouillon, wine, garlic and Italian seasoning, then cover. Reduce heat and simmer, turning every 15 minutes, for 2 hours. Add mushrooms, re-cover and simmer for ½ hour longer. Remove meat to a serving dish and keep warm. Pour meat juices from skillet into a large measuring cup. Add enough water to make 1 cup and return to skillet. Add flour dissolved in ¼ cup water and simmer over medium heat, stirring constantly, until thickened. Pour sauce over meat before serving. Serves 6.

Per serving: 184 cal. (28% from fat); 25 g protein; 5.7 g fat (2.2 g sat.); 3.3 g carbo.; 209 mg sodium; 68 mg chol.; 0.67 g fiber. Exchanges: 3 lean meat, 1 vegetable. Add ½ fat exchange to meal plan.

Stuffed Cabbage Leaves

A flavorful, satisfying entrée.

1 pound very lean ground beef
4 tablespoons grated fresh onion
1½ cups cooked rice
½ teaspoon dried dillweed
1 teaspoon dried thyme leaves
1 teaspoon Morton Lite Salt® Mixture
    Freshly ground pepper to taste
12 large cabbage leaves
3 cups tomato sauce

In a large, heavy skillet sprayed with nonstick spray, brown ground beef and onion over medium-high heat. Add rice, dillweed, thyme, Morton Lite Salt® Mixture and pepper and mix well. Cook cabbage leaves in boiling water for 1 minute. Drain and pat dry. Spoon meat mixture onto center of leaves, fold over, envelope fashion, and secure with toothpicks. Place in a shallow baking dish sprayed with nonstick spray. Pour tomato sauce over cabbage rolls, cover and bake in a preheated 325° oven for 45 minutes. Serves 6.

Per serving: 236 cal. (36% from fat); 13.4 g protein; 9.4 g fat (3.7 g sat.); 26 g carbo.; 268 mg sodium; 36 mg chol.; 0.86 g fiber. Exchanges: 1 high-fat meat, 1½ bread, 1 vegetable.

German Beef Rouladen

A unique blend of flavors!

1¼ pounds thin-cut, lean round steak, cut into 5 pieces
1 tablespoon Dijon mustard
½ cup minced fresh onion
¼ cup chopped dill pickle
¼ cup cooked, lean bacon bits
Dash freshly ground pepper
1½ cups water
1 beef bouillon cube
¼ cup flour

Between two sheets of heavy plastic wrap, pound each piece of steak to ¼" thickness. Spread mustard evenly over one side of pounded meat. Scatter onion, pickle, bacon bits and pepper over mustard. Roll up and secure with toothpicks. In a large, heavy skillet sprayed with nonstick spray, brown beef rolls over medium-high heat, turning often. Add water and bouillon cube. Cover and simmer until tender, about 45 minutes. Remove cooked beef rolls to a serving platter and keep warm. Pour remaining juice from skillet into a large measuring cup. Add enough water to make 2 cups. Pour into a blender, then add flour. Mix until smooth. Return to skillet and cook over medium heat, stirring constantly, until thickened. Pour over beef rolls. Serves 5.

Per serving: 180 cal. (29% from fat); 27 g protein: 5.7 g fat (1.9 g sat.); 3.2 g carbo.; 369 mg sodium; 71 mg chol.; 0.2 g fiber. Exchanges: 4 lean meat. Add 1½ fat exchanges to meal plan.

Italian Meatballs

Serve as an entrée or hors d'oeuvre.

1 slice French bread, crumbled
¼ cup water
1 pound very lean ground beef
1 egg
3 tablespoons each: finely chopped onion and parsley
¼ teaspoon each: Morton Lite Salt® Mixture, dried oregano leaves and garlic powder
2 tablespoons grated Parmesan cheese

Soak bread in water, then mix with remaining ingredients. Shape into 20 meatballs. Place on a baking sheet sprayed with nonstick spray and bake in a preheated 450° oven for 15 to 20 minutes, until browned and cooked through. Serves 5.

Per serving: 190 cal. (59% from fat); 13.8 g protein; 12.4 g fat (5 g sat.); 4 g carbo.; 175 mg sodium; 88 mg chol.; 0.1 g fiber. Exchanges: 1 high-fat meat, 1 medium-fat meat, ⅓ bread.

Ginger Beef

This is a great way to use leftover barbecued meat.

1½ pounds lean sirloin steak (or substitute 1½ lbs. leftover cooked meat—beef, lamb or poultry), trimmed of any fat
1 large onion, chopped
1 teaspoon finely grated fresh ginger
1½ cups each: canned tomatoes and water
½ envelope (1 oz.) onion soup mix
1 teaspoon turmeric or curry powder
Dash cayenne pepper, optional
1 tablespoon cornstarch, dissolved in ½ cup water

Cut meat into bite-size cubes. Over high heat, brown in a large, heavy skillet sprayed with nonstick spray. (Note: If using leftover cooked meat, it is not necessary to brown it.) Stir often. Remove from skillet. Respray skillet. Add onion and ginger. Cover and steam-sauté. Cook over medium-high heat until browned, stirring often. Add browned meat and remaining ingredients to skillet and cover. Cook until very tender, about 1 hour. Add more water if sauce is too thick. Serve with plain rice and chutney (see p. 120). Serves 7.

Per serving: 183 cal. (58% from fat); 13 g protein; 11.8 g fat (4.7 g sat.); 5.3 g carbo.; 171 mg sodium; 47 mg chol.; 0.74 g fiber. Exchanges: 2 medium-fat meat, 1 vegetable.

Pot Roast of Beef

Simple to fix and absolutely deli⟨

2½ pounds lean beef roast, trimmed of any fat
1 envelope (1 oz.) onion soup mix
2 cups mushrooms, sliced
Freshly ground pepper to taste

Cut a piece of heavy aluminum foil large enough to enclose the beef roast. Place the meat on top of the foil. Sprinkle soup mix, mushrooms and pepper over the meat. Carefully seal the foil. Place the packet on a large baking sheet and bake in a preheated 325° oven for 4 hours. Serve the meat juices with the cooked meat. Serves 9.

Per serving: 176 cal. (32% from fat); 27.3 g protein; 6.2 g fat (2.4 g sat.); 1.13 g carbo.; 113 mg sodium; 75 mg chol.; 0.42 g fiber. Exchanges: 4 lean meat. Add 1 fat exchange to meal plan.

Veal Scallopini

A delicately seasoned gourmet treat.

1 pound veal cutlets
½ teaspoon Original Blend
  Mrs. Dash® seasoning
1 cup sliced mushrooms
¼ cup thinly sliced green onion
1 large clove garlic, minced
½ teaspoon dried herbs (basil, rosemary
  or oregano)
1 package (1 teaspoon) chicken
  bouillon granules
2 teaspoons each: cornstarch and flour
½ cup dry white wine or dry vermouth
1 cup water
2 tablespoons chopped fresh parsley

Place veal cutlets, one at a time, between 2 heavy plastic food bags. Pound on both sides until ¼" thick. Season veal with Mrs. Dash®. In a large, heavy skillet sprayed with nonstick spray, brown cutlets on both sides over high heat. Remove from skillet and keep warm on a serving platter. Wipe out skillet and respray with nonstick spray. Stir-fry mushrooms, green onion and garlic in skillet over medium-high heat until golden. Add to skillet: dried herbs, chicken bouillon granules and cornstarch and flour mixed with wine and water. Simmer for 2 minutes, stirring constantly, until thickened. Pour sauce over cutlets and sprinkle with parsley. Serves 4.

Per serving: 217 cal. (39% from fat); 22.7 g protein; 9.3 g fat (4 g sat.); 3.9 g carbo.; 333 mg sodium; 104 mg chol.; 0.5 g fiber. Exchanges: 3 lean meat, 1 vegetable.

Veal Cordon Bleu

A "lite" version of a classic favorite.

4 1-ounce slices lean cooked ham
4 1-ounce slices fat-free Swiss cheese
4 veal cutlets (½ lb.), pounded ¼" thick
1 egg, beaten
⅓ cup fine, dry seasoned bread crumbs

Place 1 ham slice and 1 cheese slice on one half of each cutlet. Fold cutlet over to cover. Pound the edges to seal. Dip each stuffed cutlet in egg, then coat with crumbs. Place on a large baking sheet sprayed with nonstick spray. Bake in a preheated 475° oven for 5 minutes; turn cutlets over and bake for 5 minutes longer. Serves 4.

Per serving: 219 cal. (30% from fat); 28 g protein; 7.3 g fat (2.53 g sat.); 7.1 g carbo.; 624 mg sodium; 116 mg chol.; 0.33 g fiber. Exchanges: 4 lean meat, ½ bread. Add 1 fat exchange to meal plan.

Sweet & Sour Pork

A Chinese favorite that is easy to prepare.

1 pound pork tenderloin, trimmed of fat and cut into strips ½" wide and 2" long
2 tablespoons low-sodium soy sauce
1 clove garlic, minced
¾ cup pineapple juice
¼ cup rice vinegar
1 package (1 teaspoon) chicken bouillon granules
1½ tablespoons cornstarch, dissolved in ½ cup water
Sugar substitute equal to ¼ cup sugar (i.e., 1 teaspoon Sweet'N Low®)
1 cup pineapple chunks
½ each: red and green bell pepper, seeded and cut into ½" chunks

Marinate pork with soy sauce and garlic in a sealed plastic food bag for 1 hour. Meanwhile, prepare sweet and sour sauce: Combine pineapple juice, vinegar, chicken bouillon granules, dissolved cornstarch and sugar substitute in a saucepan. Cook over medium heat, stirring constantly, until thickened. Add pineapple chunks to sauce. Keep warm. In a large, heavy skillet sprayed with nonstick spray, stir-fry pork and pepper chunks over high heat until pork is cooked and peppers are crisp-tender. Add sweet and sour sauce. Stir to mix. Serves 5.

Per serving: 182 cal. (17% from fat); 20 g protein; 3.4 g fat (1.13 g sat.); 17.7 g carbo.; 298 mg sodium; 60 mg chol.; 0.79 g fiber. Exchanges: 3 lean meat, 1 fruit. Add 1 fat exchange to meal plan.

Baked Pork Chops with Potatoes

A slimmed-down entrée the family will love!

4 medium potatoes, peeled and sliced
1 small onion, sliced
½ teaspoon Morton Lite Salt® Mixture
1½ teaspoons Original Blend Mrs. Dash® seasoning
1½ pounds boneless pork chops, trimmed of fat

Mix sliced potatoes and onion. Place in a 9" by 13" casserole sprayed with nonstick spray. Sprinkle with ½ of the Morton Lite Salt® Mixture and ½ of Mrs. Dash®. Cover with aluminum foil and bake in a preheated 400° oven for 25 minutes. Remove foil and place pork chops on top of potatoes. Sprinkle with remaining Morton Lite Salt® Mixture and Mrs. Dash®. Return to 400° oven (without foil) and bake 20 minutes longer—until pork chops are thoroughly cooked and potatoes are tender. Serves 6.

Per serving: 196 cal. (18% from fat); 25 g protein; 4 g fat (1.36 g sat.); 14 g carbo.; 156 mg sodium; 75 mg chol.; 0.47 g fiber. Exchanges: 3 lean meat, 1 bread. Add 1 fat exchange to meal plan.

Pork Cutlets with Herb-Wine Sauce

Couscous with Pine Nuts (see p. 74) is a delicious accompaniment.

1 pound pork tenderloin, cut into ½" thick slices
¼ teaspoon Morton Lite Salt® Mixture
⅛ teaspoon freshly grated pepper
1 green onion (white part only), finely chopped
1 teaspoon dried rosemary
½ cup dry vermouth or white wine
2 teaspoons cornstarch, dissolved in ¼ cup water

Season pork with Morton Lite Salt® Mixture and pepper. In a large, heavy skillet sprayed with nonstick spray, brown pork slices and onion over medium-high heat. Add rosemary and wine. Cover and simmer for 5 minutes, until pork is cooked through. Remove pork and keep warm. Add dissolved cornstarch to skillet and cook, stirring constantly, until thickened. Pour sauce over pork. Serves 4.

Per serving: 155 cal. (23% from fat); 23.3 g protein; 3.9 g fat (1.34 g sat.); 0.33 g carbo.; 128 mg sodium; 75 mg chol.; 0 g fiber. Exchanges: 3½ lean meat. Add 1 fat exchange to meal plan.

Chinese Barbecued Pork

The basting sauce gives this entrée an attractive golden brown glaze.

2 pounds pork tenderloin
2 tablespoons dry sherry
3 tablespoons low-sodium soy sauce
½ teaspoon finely grated fresh ginger
Sugar substitute equal to 2 teaspoons sugar (i. e., 2 teaspoons SugarTwin®)
3 drops red food coloring, optional
1 clove garlic, minced
¼ teaspoon Chinese five-spice seasoning (or substitute ¼ teaspoon ground allspice)

Combine all ingredients in a large plastic food bag. Marinate overnight in refrigerator. Drain marinade and reserve. Roast pork on a rack in an aluminum foil-lined pan in a preheated 325° oven for 1¼ hours, or barbecue 4" to 6" above medium-hot coals, turning frequently, until done. Baste often with marinade. Cut in ⅜" thick, diagonal slices. Serves 8.

Per serving: 141 cal. (25% from fat); 24 g protein; 3.9 g fat (1.34 g sat.); 0.63 g carbo.; 83 mg sodium; 75 mg chol.; 0.02 g fiber. Exchanges: 3½ lean meat. Add 1 fat exchange to meal plan.

Stir-Fried Pork with Broccoli & Carrots

Serve this colorful stir-fried dish with plain rice.

1 pound lean pork tenderloin, cut into thin slices
2 cups broccoli florets
2 medium carrots, peeled and cut into ¼" slices
1 can (8 oz.) water chestnuts, sliced and drained
¼ cup dry sherry or white wine
¼ cup low-sodium soy sauce
1½ cups chicken broth (or use 1½ teaspoons chicken bouillon granules plus 1½ cups water)
4 teaspoons vinegar
2 tablespoons cornstarch
Sugar substitute equal to 2 tablespoons brown sugar (i.e., 2 tablespoons Brown SugarTwin®)

In a large, heavy skillet sprayed with nonstick spray, stir-fry pork slices over medium-high heat until done. In a covered saucepan, steam broccoli and carrots in a steamer basket over ½" water, until crisp-tender. Mix sherry or wine, soy sauce, chicken broth, vinegar, cornstarch and sugar substitute. Add to skillet with cooked pork and drained water chestnuts. Cook over medium heat, stirring constantly, until sauce has thickened. Add steamed vegetables. Stir gently to mix. Serves 5.

Per serving: 194 cal. (19% from fat); 24 g protein; 3.9 g fat (1.3 g sat.); 13 g carbo.; 507 mg sodium; 61 mg chol.; 1.03 g fiber. Exchanges: 3 lean meat, 1 bread. Add 1 fat exchange to meal plan.

Chinese Pork with Asparagus

An exotic blend of oriental flavors.

¼ pound pork tenderloin, cut into bite-size chunks
½ pound (about 1 cup) asparagus, cut into 1" diagonal slices (discard tough ends)
1 clove garlic, minced
¼ cup sliced green onion
1 tablespoon low-sodium soy sauce
1 teaspoon sesame oil
1 package (1 teaspoon) chicken bouillon granules
½ teaspoon Chinese five-spice seasoning (or substitute ½ teaspoon ground allspice)
1 tablespoon cornstarch, dissolved in ⅔ cup water

In a heavy skillet sprayed with nonstick spray, stir-fry pork over high heat until browned. Remove from pan and keep warm. Respray skillet and add asparagus, garlic and green onion. Spray vegetables with nonstick spray. Cover skillet and cook over medium heat, stirring occasionally, until asparagus is crisp-tender. Add meat and remaining ingredients to skillet. Cook over medium heat, stirring constantly, until sauce has thickened. Serve with plain rice. Serves 2.

Per serving: 148 cal. (29% from fat); 15.7 g protein; 4.7 g fat (1.14 g sat.); 10.6 g carbo.; 449 mg sodium; 38 mg chol.; 1.25 g fiber. Exchanges: 1½ lean meat, 2 vegetable.

Ham Caribbean

This dish abounds with tropical flavor.

2 pounds lean ham steak, trimmed of any fat
⅓ cup orange juice concentrate
1 teaspoon ground cloves
1 teaspoon rum extract, optional
2 teaspoons cornstarch, dissolved in 3 tablespoons water
1 cup unsweetened crushed pineapple with juice
½ cup raisins
Sugar substitute equal to ¼ cup brown sugar (i.e., ½ cup Brown SugarTwin®)

Bake ham in a preheated 350° oven for 30 minutes in a shallow baking dish sprayed with nonstick spray. In a saucepan, combine orange juice concentrate, cloves, rum extract (if used), dissolved cornstarch and pineapple with juice. Simmer over medium heat, stirring constantly, until thickened. Stir in raisins and sugar substitute. Serve warm over baked ham. Serves 8.

Per serving: 157 cal. (20% from fat); 16.5 g protein; 3.55 g fat (1.16 g sat.); 14.7 g carbo.; 1,031 mg sodium; 37 mg chol.; 0.93 g fiber. Exchanges: 2 lean meat, 1 fruit. Add ½ fat exchange to meal plan.

Middle Eastern Braised Lamb

Slow simmering blends the rich flavors.

5 cloves garlic, minced
1" piece peeled fresh ginger, finely grated
2 pounds lean, boneless leg of lamb, cut into 1" cubes
1 cup chopped onion
1 cup peeled, chopped tomatoes
1 teaspoon Morton Lite Salt® Mixture
2 teaspoons each: ground cumin and ground coriander
⅛ teaspoon cayenne pepper
1 cup water
1¼ pounds fresh spinach, washed and with stems removed
1 tablespoon toasted pine nuts*

Mix garlic and ginger with lamb cubes. In a large, heavy skillet sprayed with nonstick spray, brown lamb mixture and onion, stirring often. Add tomatoes, Morton Lite Salt® Mixture, cumin, coriander, cayenne pepper and water. Cover tightly and simmer for 1 hour, or until lamb is tender. Scatter spinach over cooked meat. Cover and simmer for 3 minutes longer. Transfer stew to a heated serving dish and sprinkle with pine nuts. Serves 8.
*To toast, bake at 300° on an ungreased baking sheet until golden.

Per serving: 208 cal. (37% from fat); 27.3 g protein; 8.5 g fat (3.24 g sat.); 6.1 g carbo.; 309 mg sodium; 53 mg chol.; 3.6 g fiber. Exchanges: 3½ lean meat, 1 vegetable.

Lamb Shish Kabobs

Serve with Onion-Rice Pilaf (see p. 74).

1 pound boneless leg of lamb, trimmed of all fat and cut into 1¼" cubes
¼ cup dry sherry or red wine
¼ cup fat-free Italian salad dressing
½ teaspoon dried rosemary or oregano
2 large cloves garlic, minced
8 small boiling onions, peeled
1 green bell pepper, seeded and cut into 1¼" cubes
8 large mushrooms
8 large cherry tomatoes

Marinate lamb cubes with wine, salad dressing, rosemary or oregano, and garlic in a sealed plastic food bag overnight. Steam onions until barely tender. Remove meat from marinade and reserve marinade. Arrange meat on skewers, alternating with onions, pepper cubes and mushrooms. Barbecue 6" above coals for 15 minutes, basting with marinade and turning occasionally. Add cherry tomatoes to the skewer ends, baste and barbecue for 5 minutes longer. Serves 4.

Per serving: 224 cal. (31% from fat); 26.4 g protein; 7.7 g fat (3.1 g sat.); 10 g carbo.; 230 mg sodium; 53 mg chol.; 2.7 g fiber. Exchanges: 3 lean meat, 2 vegetable.

Serbian Crockpot Lamb

Full of intriguing flavors and easy to prepare.

1 small cabbage, thinly sliced
½ medium onion, thinly sliced
5 medium cloves garlic, minced
1 teaspoon dried thyme leaves
6 medium red potatoes, cut into ½" thick slices
2 teaspoons Original Blend Mrs. Dash® seasoning
2 pounds boned leg of lamb with all fat removed
¼ cup red wine vinegar
3 tablespoons finely chopped fresh parsley

Mix together cabbage, onion, garlic, thyme, potatoes and Mrs. Dash®. Cut lamb into 9 serving-size pieces. Spray a large Crockpot with nonstick spray. Layer cabbage mixture alternately with lamb slices. Cover and cook on low for 8 to 10 hours or on high for 4 to 5 hours (or bake in a tightly covered casserole in a preheated 300° oven for 4 to 5 hours). Before serving, pour vinegar over cooked cabbage and lamb. Let stand for 15 minutes. Garnish each serving with chopped parsley. Serves 9.

Per serving: 241 cal. (46% from fat); 15 g protein; 12.2 g fat (4.8 g sat.); 17 g carbo.; 64 mg sodium; 48 mg chol.; 0.61 g fiber. Exchanges: 2 medium-fat meat, 1 bread, ½ fat.

Fish & Shellfish

Stuffed Fillets of Sole with Newburg Sauce

Elegant, yet easy to prepare.

SOLE:

- 5 fillets of sole (about 1 pound total)
- 1 egg white
- 2 tablespoons nonfat milk powder
- ⅛ teaspoon Morton Lite Salt® Mixture
- 1 teaspoon dried parsley flakes
- 1 drop hot pepper sauce
- ½ cup water
- ½ cup dry white wine
- ½ small onion, sliced
- 1 slice lemon
- 1 bay leaf
- 3 whole peppercorns
- ¼ teaspoon dried tarragon leaves

NEWBURG SAUCE:

- 1 package (1 teaspoon) chicken bouillon granules
- 2 tablespoons each: flour and dry sherry
- ¾ cup fish stock (from simmered fillets of sole)
- 1 egg yolk
- 2 tablespoons nonfat milk powder
  Dash paprika
- ½ teaspoon Original Blend Mrs. Dash® seasoning

To prepare sole: Select the 4 best fish fillets and set aside. Cut the remaining fillet into 1" pieces. Place pieces in a blender or food processor with egg white, milk powder, Morton Lite Salt® Mixture, parsley flakes and hot pepper sauce. Blend until mixture is smooth. Spread the fish mixture over the 4 reserved fish fillets (about 2 rounded tablespoons each), and roll up fillets. Fasten with toothpicks. In a large skillet, mix water, wine, onion, lemon slice, bay leaf, peppercorns and tarragon leaves. Place fish rolls in skillet and cover. Simmer for 10 minutes. Remove cooked fish rolls and keep warm on serving platter. Reserve and strain ¾ cup fish stock. Allow to cool slightly.

To make sauce: Mix all sauce ingredients in blender, then simmer in a small saucepan, stirring constantly, until thickened. Pour sauce over fish rolls. Serves 4.

Per serving: 168 cal. (15% from fat); 24.4 g protein; 2.86 g fat (0.78 g sat.); 4 g carbo.; 443 mg sodium; 114 mg chol.; 0.05 g fiber. Exchanges: 3½ lean meat. Add 1½ fat exchange to meal plan.

Baked Fish with Saffron & Red Bell Pepper

A special-occasion dish your guests will appreciate.

1 large red bell pepper, cut into ½" pieces
3 large cloves garlic, minced
¼ teaspoon crumbled saffron threads
Cayenne pepper to taste
½ teaspoon dried, crumbled thyme leaves
2 pounds sea bass, cod, scrod or halibut fillets, cut ½" to ¾" thick
2 teaspoons each: flour and cornstarch
1 cup dry white wine
2 packages (1 teaspoon each) chicken bouillon granules
2 tablespoons chopped fresh parsley

In a large, heavy skillet sprayed with nonstick spray, stir-fry bell pepper and garlic over medium-high heat until soft. Stir in saffron, cayenne pepper and thyme. Place fish fillets in a single layer in a large baking dish sprayed with nonstick spray. Spoon bell pepper mixture over fillets. Cover with aluminum foil and bake in a preheated 400° oven for 15 minutes, or until fish flakes. Place fish on a serving platter and keep warm. Return any juices to the skillet. Mix flour, cornstarch, wine and chicken bouillon granules and add to skillet. Cook over medium heat, stirring constantly, until thickened. Pour sauce over fish fillets. Sprinkle with parsley. Serves 8.

Per serving: 151 cal. (23% from fat); 20.8 g protein; 3.85 g fat (0.78 g sat.); 2.43 g carbo.; 666 mg sodium; 58 mg chol.; 0.23 g fiber. Exchanges: 3 lean meat. Add 1 fat exchange to meal plan.

Sesame Fillets of Sole

Delicate flavor with an oriental accent.

4 teaspoons sesame seeds
1 pound fillet of sole or orange roughy fillets
1 egg white, beaten
1 teaspoon each: sesame oil and lemon juice
1 teaspoon finely grated fresh ginger
2 tablespoons low-sodium soy sauce
1½ teaspoons cornstarch, dissolved in ½ cup water
1 small green onion, sliced

Toast sesame seeds in a large, heavy skillet over medium heat, stirring constantly, until golden. Remove from skillet. Dip fish fillets in beaten egg white, then sprinkle with toasted sesame seeds. Heat skillet over medium-high heat and spray with nonstick spray. Add 2 of the fillets and cook for 2 to 3 minutes. Carefully turn fillets with a spatula and cook until done, 1 to 2 minutes longer. Remove fish to a heated serving dish. Repeat with remaining fillets. To prepare sauce, simmer remaining ingredients in a small saucepan over medium heat, stirring constantly, until thickened. Serve sauce in small bowls for dipping. Serves 4.

Per serving: 142 cal. (25% from fat); 23.4 g protein; 3.95 g fat (0.67 g sat.); 2.2 g carbo.; 144 mg sodium; 59 mg chol.; 0.03 g fiber. Exchanges: 3½ lean meat. Add 1 fat exchange to meal plan.

Crusty Oven-Fried Fish

With a crispy, crunchy coating that tastes great!

2 pounds fish fillets
1 egg, beaten with 2 tablespoons milk
½ cup fine, dry seasoned bread crumbs

Line a large cookie sheet with aluminum foil. Spray with nonstick spray. Dip each fish fillet into the egg mixture and then coat with bread crumbs. Place on the foil, leaving a space between each fillet. Bake in a preheated 500° oven for 5 minutes (for ½" thick fillets) or 10 minutes (for 1" thick fillets). Serves 6.

Per serving: 213 cal. (15% from fat); 31 g protein; 3.44 g fat (0.92 g sat.); 12.3 g carbo.; 351 mg sodium; 116 mg chol.; 0.67 g fiber. Exchanges: 4 lean meat, 1 bread. Add 1½ fat exchanges to meal plan.

Curried Fish Fillets

Quick to fix and very low in fat.

1½ pounds fish fillets, cut into 6 portions
1 cup plain nonfat yogurt
2 tablespoons lemon juice
2 teaspoons curry powder
½ teaspoon garlic powder

Place fish fillets in a large plastic food bag. Mix remaining ingredients and pour into bag. Coat all surfaces of fish with marinade. Seal bag and refrigerate for 1 to 2 hours. Drain fish and discard marinade. Place fish in a shallow baking dish sprayed with nonstick spray. Bake in a preheated 450° oven until fish flakes easily with a fork (allow 4 to 6 minutes per ½" thickness of fish). Serves 6.

Per serving: 131 cal. (11% from fat); 25 g protein; 1.56 g fat (0.32 g sat.); 3 g carbo.; 77 mg sodium; 41 mg chol.; 0 g fiber. Exchanges: 3½ lean meat. Add 2 fat exchanges to meal plan.

Red Snapper Veracruz

Salsa and grated cheese flavor this dish.

1½ pounds red snapper fillets
1½ cups salsa (mild or hot)
⅔ cup grated fat-free cheddar, jack or mozzarella cheese

Place snapper fillets in a large, shallow baking dish sprayed with nonstick spray. Pour salsa over fillets. Bake uncovered in a preheated 400° oven for 15 to 20 minutes, or until fish flakes. Remove from oven and sprinkle with grated cheese. Return to oven for 3 minutes to melt cheese. Serves 8.

Per serving: 105 cal. (11% from fat); 20.5 g protein; 1.27 g fat (0.25 g sat.); 2.3 g carbo.; 105 mg sodium; 32 mg chol.; 0.38 g fiber. Exchanges: 3 lean meat. Add 1½ fat exchanges to meal plan.

Quick Seafood Paella

Saffron adds a subtle, intriguing flavor.

1 pound medium shrimp, shelled and deveined
1 large clove garlic, minced
1 small onion, chopped
2 cups water
2 packages (1 teaspoon each) chicken bouillon granules
1 cup long grain rice
1 can (6 oz.) minced clams with juice
½ teaspoon crumbled saffron threads, optional
1 small red bell pepper, cut into ½" pieces
1 can (16 oz.) artichoke hearts, drained and cut into 1" pieces
½ cup frozen peas, thawed

In a large, heavy skillet sprayed heavily with nonstick spray, stir-fry shrimp over medium-high heat until cooked—about 5 minutes. Remove from skillet. Respray skillet with nonstick spray and stir-fry garlic and onion until tender—about 5 minutes. Add water and bring to a boil. Stir in chicken bouillon granules, rice, clams with juice, saffron (if used) and red bell pepper. Cover tightly, and simmer for 15 minutes. Stir in artichoke hearts and peas. Cook 5 minutes longer. Gently mix in cooked shrimp. Serves 6.

Per serving: 231 cal. (8% from fat); 22.6 g protein; 2.16 g fat (0.42 g sat.); 33.5 g carbo.; 714 mg sodium; 123 mg chol.; 2.25 g fiber. Exchanges: 2½ lean meat, 2 bread. Add 1 fat exchange to meal plan.

Oriental Steamed Fish

Fish served with a light oriental sauce.

3 onion slices
2 teaspoons finely grated fresh ginger, divided
1 cup water
1¾ pounds orange roughy, turbot or large sole fillets
2 teaspoons sesame oil
3 tablespoons low-sodium soy sauce
3 green onions, chopped

To a large steamer pot, add onion slices, 1 teaspoon ginger and water. Add steamer basket. Place fish on steamer basket sprayed with nonstick spray. Cover and simmer for 5 to 15 minutes (depending on the thickness of the fish) until fish flakes. Remove fish to a heated platter and pour over it sauce made from mixture of 1 teaspoon ginger, sesame oil and soy sauce. Garnish with green onions. Serves 5.

Per serving: 244 cal. (51% from fat); 26.3 g protein; 13.7 g fat (0.54 g sat.); 1.34 g carbo.; 165 mg sodium; 34 mg chol.; 0.08 g fiber. Exchanges: 3½ lean meat, ½ fat.

Garlic Shrimp with Oriental Vegetables

A delicious blend of flavors, colors and textures.

¾ pound large shrimp, shelled and deveined

2 cloves garlic, minced

⅔ cup fresh mushrooms, washed and sliced

4 green onions, cut into 2" julienne strips

1 can (8 oz.) water chestnuts, drained and sliced

⅔ cup edible pea pods, tough ends and strings removed

1 tablespoon cornstarch, dissolved in ½ cup water

¼ cup dry white wine

1 tablespoon oyster sauce

1 package (1 teaspooon) chicken bouillon granules

2 tablespoons low-sodium soy sauce

1 teaspoon sesame oil
Sugar substitute equal to ½ teaspoon sugar (i.e., ½ teaspoon SugarTwin®)

In a large, heavy skillet sprayed heavily with nonstick spray, stir-fry shrimp and 1 clove minced garlic over medium-high heat. When cooked, remove from skillet and keep warm. Respray skillet with nonstick spray. Add remaining garlic, mushrooms and green onions. Cook over medium-high heat, stirring often. Cover to steam-sauté if vegetables become too dry. Remove from skillet when crisp-tender and keep warm with shrimp. Add remaining ingredients to skillet and cook, stirring constantly, until pea pods are crisp-tender and sauce is thickened. Stir in shrimp and vegetables. Serve with plain rice. Serves 3.

Per serving: 196 cal. (17% from fat); 26.4 g protein; 3.75 g fat (0.63 g sat.); 15.2 g carbo.; 478 mg sodium; 173 mg chol.; 3.2 g fiber. Exchanges: 3½ lean meat, 1 bread. Add 1 fat exchange to meal plan.

Grilled Fish Steaks

A versatile dish that is especially good with Coleslaw (see p. 26).

3 tablespoons low-sodium soy sauce

2 tablespoons lemon juice
Sugar substitute equal to 1 tablespoon sugar (i.e., 1 tablespoon SugarTwin®)

2 teaspoons finely grated fresh ginger

1 clove garlic, minced

⅛ teaspoon freshly ground pepper

2 pounds halibut, shark or sea bass steaks, ¾" thick
Lemon wedges

In a large, shallow casserole dish, mix soy sauce, lemon juice, sugar substitute, ginger, garlic and pepper. Add fish and turn to coat with marinade. Chill for 1 to 2 hours, turning occasionally. Barbecue fish 4" to 6" above hot coals, turning once, for 8 minutes. Garnish with lemon wedges. Serves 6.

Per serving: 167 cal. (18% from fat); 31.6 g protein; 3.4 g fat (0.48 g sat.); 0.66 g carbo.; 106 mg sodium; 48 mg chol.; 0.02 g fiber. Exchanges: 4½ lean meat. Add 2 fat exchanges to meal plan.

Scallops with Pea Pods

The delicately seasoned sauce is a gourmet treat.

1 pound bay scallops (or sea scallops, cut into ¼" slices)
¼ teaspoon sesame oil
⅛ teaspoon ground pepper
½ teaspoon finely grated fresh ginger (or ¼ teaspoon ground ginger)
1 cup edible pea pods, with ends and strings removed
1 large clove garlic, minced
¾ cup (8 oz. can) sliced bamboo shoots, drained
2 green onions, cut into 2" pieces
1 tablespoon cornstarch
1 cup chicken bouillon
1 tablespoon oyster sauce, optional

Combine scallops with sesame oil and pepper in a small bowl. Marinate 30 minutes. In a large, heavy skillet sprayed with nonstick spray, stir-fry scallops over medium-high heat until they are opaque. (Do not crowd scallops in skillet while cooking.) Remove skillet from burner. In a medium, heavy skillet sprayed with nonstick spray, cover and cook ginger, pea pods, garlic, bamboo shoots and green onions over medium-high heat until barely tender, stirring occasionally. Remove skillet from burner and add cooked scallops. Mix cornstarch with bouillon and oyster sauce (if used). Add to (now empty) scallop skillet, and cook over medium heat, stirring constantly, until sauce is thickened. Gently stir cooked scallops and vegetables into thickened sauce. Serve immediately. Serves 4.

Per serving: 148 cal. (10% from fat); 21 g protein; 1.65 g fat (0.25 g sat.); 11.8 g carbo.; 466 mg sodium; 38.5 mg chol.; 1.85 g fiber. Exchanges: 2½ lean meat, 1 bread. Add 1 fat exchange to meal plan.

Olive-Salmon Loaf

Serve with fat-free Tartar Sauce (see p. 89).

2 cans (14.75 oz. each) canned salmon, drained
3 tablespoons sliced black olives
1½ cups bread cubes
½ cup nonfat milk
2 eggs, beaten
2 tablespoons grated fresh onion
2 tablespoons minced fresh parsley
2 tablespoons lemon juice
½ teaspoon Morton Lite Salt® Mixture
Freshly ground pepper to taste

Remove any skin and bones from salmon and discard. Mix salmon with remaining ingredients. Pour mixture into a loaf pan sprayed with nonstick spray. Bake in a preheated 375° oven for 40 minutes. Serves 5.

Per serving: 260 cal. (43% from fat); 24 g protein; 12.5 g fat (2.8 g sat.); 11.7 g carbo.; 667 mg sodium; 146 mg chol.; 0.79 g fiber. Exchanges: 3 lean meat, 1 bread, ½ fat.

Tuna-Mushroom Casserole

This well-seasoned dish can be prepared in advance.

2 cups low-fat (1% fat) milk
4 tablespoons flour
1 package (1 teaspoon) chicken bouillon granules
2 cups cooked (4 oz. uncooked) egg noodles
1 can (6 oz.) water-packed tuna, drained
2 hard-boiled eggs, shelled and cut into ¼" thick slices
1 can (6 oz.) sliced mushrooms, drained
1 can (3 oz.) pimientos, drained and chopped
½ cup grated fat-free cheddar cheese (2 oz.)

Mix milk, flour and chicken bouillon granules in blender. Pour into a large, heavy saucepan and simmer over medium heat, stirring constantly, until thickened. Remove from heat and add remaining ingredients. Stir gently to mix. Bake in a preheated 350° oven for 30 minutes, or until hot. Serves 7.

Per serving: 178 cal. (16% from fat); 16 g protein; 3.2 g fat (1 g sat.); 20 g carbo.; 444 mg sodium; 79 mg chol.; 1.4 g fiber. Exchanges: 1½ lean meat, 1 bread, 1 vegetable.

Tuna with Curried Rice

Satisfying enough for hearty appetites.

3 cups low-fat (1% fat) milk
6 tablespoons flour
½ teaspoon paprika
4 drops hot pepper sauce
1 teaspoon Worcestershire sauce
1 package (1 teaspoon) chicken bouillon granules
2 medium tomatoes, peeled and chopped
1 clove garlic, minced
2 cans (6 oz. each) water-packed tuna, drained
½ teaspoon curry powder
¼ cup slivered, toasted almonds*
3 cups hot cooked rice

In blender, mix milk with flour, paprika, hot pepper sauce, Worcestershire sauce and chicken bouillon granules. Pour milk mixture into a heavy saucepan. Add tomatoes and garlic. Cook over medium heat, stirring constantly, until thickened. Add tuna and simmer, covered, for 10 minutes. Meanwhile, mix curry powder and almonds with hot rice. Serve tuna mixture over rice. Sprinkle with additional paprika. Serves 6.

*To toast, bake at 300° on an ungreased baking sheet until golden.

Per serving: 317 cal. (18% from fat); 26 g protein; 6.3 g fat (1.6 g sat.); 37.5 g carbo.; 453 mg sodium; 42 mg chol.; 2 g fiber. Exchanges: 2 lean meat, ½ nonfat milk, 2 bread.

Chicken & Turkey

Crispy Oven-Fried Chicken

A low-calorie favorite.

⅓ cup fine, dry seasoned bread crumbs
3 tablespoons flour
½ teaspoon Morton Lite Salt® Mixture
1 egg, beaten
2 tablespoons nonfat milk
1 pound boneless, skinless
chicken breasts

In a plastic food bag, mix crumbs, flour and Morton Lite Salt® Mixture. In a shallow bowl, mix egg with milk. Dip each chicken breast into egg mixture, then into crumb mixture. Place coated chicken on baking sheet sprayed with nonstick spray. Bake in a preheated 425° oven, turning once, for 25 minutes. Serves 4.

Per serving: 150 cal. (14% from fat); 17 g protein; 2.25 g fat (0.64 g sat.); 4.6 g carbo.; 266 mg sodium; 88 mg chol.; 0.25 g fiber. Exchanges: 2 lean meat, ⅓ bread, 1 fat.

Basque Chicken

Quick to prepare, high in flavor and low in fat.

1 green bell pepper, seeded and cut into strips
½ medium onion, thinly sliced
2 cloves garlic, minced
8 ounces mushrooms, washed and sliced
2 pounds boneless, skinless chicken breasts
½ teaspoon Original Blend Mrs. Dash® seasoning, divided
6 slices (⅔ oz. each) fat-free Swiss cheese

In a large, heavy skillet sprayed heavily with nonstick spray, stir-fry pepper, onion and garlic over medium-high heat until crisp-tender. Cover skillet so that vegetables do not become too dry. Remove from skillet and keep warm in a preheated 300° oven. Respray skillet with nonstick spray and stir-fry mushrooms over medium-high heat. Remove from skillet and keep warm with pepper, onion and garlic. Mix ½ Mrs. Dash® with cooked vegetables. Respray skillet and cook chicken breasts on both sides until browned and cooked through—about 5 minutes per side. Sprinkle with remaining Mrs. Dash®. To serve: top each chicken breast with cooked vegetables, then with a slice of cheese. Heat in 300° oven until cheese melts over vegetables. Serves 6.

Per serving: 208 cal. (9% from fat); 29.7 g protein; 2.05 g fat (0.54 g sat.); 2.6 g carbo.; 236 mg sodium; 94 mg chol.; 0.7 g fiber. Exchanges: 4 lean meat, 2 fat.

Chicken-Almond Tetrazzini

Chicken in a rich-tasting, creamy sauce.

3 cups low-fat (1% fat) milk
6 tablespoons flour
2 tablespoons dried, minced onion
½ teaspoon garlic powder
3 packages (1 teaspoon each) chicken bouillon granules
¼ cup grated Parmesan cheese
⅓ cup dry white wine
7 ounces spaghetti, cooked according to package directions and drained
1½ cups cooked chicken or turkey, cut into small cubes
1 package (10 oz.) frozen chopped broccoli, steamed until barely tender
1 can (4 oz.) sliced mushrooms and juice
¼ cup pimiento, chopped
¼ cup sliced almonds

In a blender, mix milk, flour, onion, garlic powder and chicken bouillon granules. Pour into a large, heavy saucepan and cook over medium heat, stirring constantly, until thickened. Add cheese, wine, spaghetti, chicken or turkey, broccoli, mushrooms and juice and pimiento. Stir gently to mix. Pour into a large casserole dish and top with almonds. Bake in a preheated 350° oven for 40 minutes, or until thoroughly heated. Serves 7.

Per serving: 297 cal. (18% from fat); 18 g protein; 6 g fat (1.8 g sat.); 37 g carbo.; 556 mg sodium; 32 mg chol.; 3.8 g fiber. Exchanges: 1½ lean meat, 2 bread, 1 vegetable, ⅓ nonfat milk, ½ fat.

Tandoori Chicken

Turkey breast cutlets may be substituted for chicken.

3 pounds boneless, skinless chicken breasts
1 cup plain nonfat yogurt
1 teaspoon each: Morton Lite Salt® Mixture, pepper, paprika, dried ginger and curry powder
2 tablespoons lemon juice
½ teaspoon red food coloring, optional
3 cloves garlic, minced

Mix all ingredients. Marinate chicken in refrigerator for 8 hours or overnight. Remove chicken from marinade and place on aluminum foil-lined cookie sheet sprayed with nonstick spray. Bake in a preheated 425° oven for 35 minutes, or barbecue 5" from hot coals for 10 to 15 minutes, turning once. Serve with Onion-Rice Pilaf (see p. 74). Serves 9.

Per serving: 156 cal. (9% from fat); 20.6 g protein; 1.62 g fat (0.43 g sat.); 1.78 g carbo.; 302 mg sodium; 76 mg chol.; 0 g fiber. Exchanges: 3 lean meat, 2 fat.

Creamy Parmesan Chicken

A delicious way to use leftover chicken or turkey.

1   cup low-fat (1% fat) milk
½   cup white wine (or substitute ½ cup
    low-fat milk)
1   package (1 teaspoon) chicken
    bouillon granules
3   tablespoons flour
¼   cup grated Parmesan cheese
½   pound cooked chicken or turkey breast,
    cut into ½" cubes
2   tablespoons slivered, toasted almonds*

Mix milk, wine, chicken bouillon granules and flour together in a blender. Pour into a heavy saucepan and cook, stirring constantly, over medium heat until thickened. Stir in Parmesan cheese and chicken or turkey. Serve over plain rice or pasta. Sprinkle almonds over top to garnish. Serves 3.

*To toast, bake at 300° on an ungreased baking sheet until golden.

Per serving: 240 cal. (27% from fat); 19 g protein; 7.1 g fat (2.44 g sat); 11 g carbo.; 623 mg sodium; 54 mg chol.; 0.95 g fiber. Exchanges: 2 lean meat, ⅓ bread, ½ nonfat milk.

Chicken Olé

This is as colorful as it is delicious!

1   cup each: tomato sauce and
    orange juice
2   cloves garlic, minced
3   tablespoons canned chili peppers
1   package (1 teaspoon) chicken
    bouillon granules
1   teaspoon each: finely grated orange rind
    and ground cinnamon
½   teaspoon each: dried thyme leaves,
    crumbled, and Morton Lite
    Salt® Mixture
¼   cup dry sherry
2   pounds boneless, skinless
    chicken breasts
1   large onion, chopped
1   each: red and green bell pepper, seeded
    and sliced
2   tablespoons cornstarch, dissolved in
    3 tablespoons water

Mix tomato sauce, orange juice, garlic, chili peppers, chicken bouillon granules, orange rind, cinnamon, thyme, Morton Lite Salt® Mixture and sherry. Place chicken in a large skillet or casserole (suitable for stovetop and oven cooking) sprayed with nonstick spray. Scatter onion over chicken. Pour sauce mixture over top. Cover and bake in a pre-heated 350° oven for 35 minutes. Add sliced peppers, cover, and bake 15 minutes longer—until peppers are barely tender. Gently transfer chicken and peppers with a slotted spoon to a warm serving platter. Add dissolved cornstarch to chicken sauce. Cook over stovetop burner on medium heat, stirring constantly, until thickened. Pour over chicken. Serves 8.

Per serving: 176 cal. (9% from fat); 18 g protein; 1.76 g fat (0.44 g sat.); 11.2 g carbo.; 458 mg sodium; 66 mg chol.; 1 g fiber. Exchanges: 2 lean meat, 1 vegetable, ½ fruit. Add 1 fat exchange to meal plan.

Mexican Chicken

A light, spicy entrée.

1 pound boneless, skinless chicken breasts
¾ cup enchilada sauce
1 cup chicken broth
1½ tablespoons cornstarch, dissolved in ½ cup water
1 green onion, thinly sliced
¼ cup grated fat-free cheddar cheese

Place chicken in a large, ovenproof skillet sprayed with nonstick spray. Combine enchilada sauce and chicken broth and pour over chicken. Bake uncovered in a preheated 400° oven, turning once, for 35 minutes. Remove chicken to a warm serving platter. Add dissolved cornstarch to sauce in skillet. Cook on a stovetop burner, stirring constantly, over medium heat until thickened. Add water if sauce is too thick. Pour sauce over chicken and garnish with green onion slices and grated cheese. Serves 4.

Per serving: 156 cal. (13% from fat); 18.3 g protein; 2.3 g fat (0.41 g sat.); 5.5 g carbo.; 630 mg sodium; 63 mg chol.; 0.76 g fiber. Exchanges: 2 lean meat, ⅓ bread. Add ½ fat exchange to meal plan.

Easy Enchilada Casserole

A great-tasting dish—good for entertaining.

1 pound ground turkey breast
1 medium onion, chopped
2 cups each: tomato sauce and enchilada sauce
1 can (15 oz.) pinto beans and juice
12 corn tortillas
3 cups grated fat-free cheddar cheese (10 oz.)
½ cup sliced black olives

In a large, heavy skillet sprayed with nonstick spray, brown ground turkey and chopped onion over medium-high heat, stirring constantly. Add tomato sauce, enchilada sauce and beans with juice. Heat until simmering. Put a layer of meat sauce in a large casserole sprayed with nonstick spray. Add a single layer of 3 tortillas. Add another layer of meat sauce. Cover with ¼ of the cheese and olives. Repeat three more layers of 3 tortillas, meat sauce, cheese and olives. Bake in a preheated 325° oven for 50 to 60 minutes, or until hot. Serves 10.

Per serving: 266 cal. (22% from fat); 24.4 g protein; 6.5 g fat (0.78 g sat.); 26.5 g carbo.; 1,021 mg sodium; 33 mg chol.; 6.7 g fiber. Exchanges: 2½ lean meat, 1½ bread.

Armenian Chicken

Full of flavor and easy to prepare.

1 small onion, chopped
½ cup dry sherry
1 cup each: tomato juice and water
2 packages (1 teaspoon each) chicken bouillon granules
1 teaspoon paprika
⅛ teaspoon freshly ground pepper
1 large clove garlic, minced
1½ pounds boneless, skinless chicken breasts
2 tablespoons cornstarch, dissolved in ½ cup water

Mix onion, sherry, tomato juice, water, chicken bouillon granules, paprika, pepper and garlic in a large, heavy ovenproof skillet. Add chicken breasts. Bake uncovered in a preheated 400° oven, turning once, for 35 minutes. Remove chicken to a warm serving platter. Add dissolved cornstarch to liquid in skillet. Cook on a stovetop burner, stirring constantly, over medium heat, until thickened. Add more water if sauce is too thick. Pour sauce over chicken. Serves 6.

Per serving: 167 cal. (9% from fat); 17 g protein; 1.64 g fat (0.43 g sat.); 2.34 g carbo.; 514 mg sodium; 66 mg chol.; 0.32 g fiber. Exchanges: 2 lean meat, ½ vegetable. Add 1 fat exchange to meal plan.

Chicken-Almond Stir-Fry

Serve with plain rice.

1 cup each: coarsely chopped celery and onion
1 pound boneless, skinless chicken breasts, cut into ½" cubes
½ package (10 oz.) frozen peas, thawed
1 can (8 oz.) sliced water chestnuts, drained
½ red bell pepper, seeded and cut into ½" pieces
1 cup water
2 packages (1 teaspoon each) chicken bouillon granules
3 tablespoons low-sodium soy sauce
1 teaspoon sesame oil
2 tablespoons cornstarch, dissolved in ½ cup water
¼ cup slivered, toasted almonds*

In a large, heavy skillet sprayed with nonstick spray, stir-fry celery and onion over medium heat until crisp-tender. Remove from skillet. Respray skillet with nonstick spray and brown chicken over high heat, stirring constantly. Return celery and onion to skillet. Add peas, water chestnuts, bell pepper, water, chicken bouillon granules, soy sauce and sesame oil. Simmer for 3 minutes. Stir in dissolved cornstarch and cook until thickened. Garnish top with slivered almonds. Serves 5.

*To toast, bake at 300° on an ungreased baking sheet until golden.

Per serving: 202 cal. (25% from fat); 16 g protein; 5.7 g fat (0.75 g sat.); 13.6 g carbo.; 470 mg sodium; 48 mg chol.; 3.5 mg fiber. Exchanges: 2 lean meat, ½ bread, 1 vegetable.

Roast Turkey Breast with Herb Stuffing

An elegant dish your guests will love.

2 pounds whole, boned turkey breast
¼ cup chopped fresh parsley
2 teaspoons dried thyme leaves
½ teaspoon Morton Lite Salt® Mixture
⅛ teaspoon freshly ground pepper
½ cup grated fat-free mozzarella cheese
2 ounces lean ham, chopped
½ cup white wine
2 tablespoons cornstarch
1½ cups water
1 package (1 teaspoon) chicken bouillon granules

Lay 3 clean cotton strings, each about 24 inches long, across a large roasting pan sprayed with nonstick spray. Set turkey breast, skin side down, over strings. Sprinkle turkey with parsley, thyme, Morton Lite Salt® Mixture, pepper, cheese and ham. Shape turkey breast into a roll and tie with strings. Turn roast over, so that skin side is up. Insert thermometer into center. Bake in a preheated 325° oven for 1 to 1½ hours (or until thermometer reads 170°). Place on a serving platter and keep warm for 10 minutes. Mix wine with cornstarch, water and chicken bouillon granules. Add to pan drippings. Cook over medium-high heat, stirring constantly, until thickened. Pour sauce into serving bowl for spooning over slices of meat. Serves 10.

Per serving: 133 cal. (6% from fat); 25 g protein; 0.96 g fat (0.3 g sat.); 2.16 g carbo.; 319 mg sodium; 59 mg chol.; 0.05 g fiber. Exchanges: 3½ lean meat. Add 2 fat exchanges to meal plan.

Grilled Turkey Skewers

Quick to fix and very low-calorie!

1 pound turkey breast, cut into 1" cubes
1 tablespoon Dijon mustard
3 tablespoons fat-free Italian salad dressing
1 large clove garlic, minced
½ teaspoon Original Blend Mrs. Dash® seasoning

Mix all ingredients and let marinate for at least 1 hour, preferably 4 hours or more. Place marinated turkey cubes on 4 skewers. Barbecue 5" from coals for 5 minutes per side, or until cooked through. Serves 4.

Per serving: 133 cal. (6% from fat); 27.6 g protein; 0.89 g fat (0.23 g sat.); 0.97 g carbo.; 231 mg sodium; 70 mg chol.; 0.02 g fiber. Exchanges: 4 lean meat. Add 2 fat exchanges to meal plan.

Hearty Turkey Chili

For convenience, this dish can be prepared in advance.

2 pounds ground turkey
1 cup chopped onion
1 large clove garlic, minced
⅓ cup finely chopped fresh parsley, optional
2 cans (16 oz. each) tomatoes (with juice), cut up
1 can (8 oz.) tomato sauce
2 cans (15 oz. each) kidney, pinto or pink beans, drained
1 green bell pepper, seeded and chopped
1 tablespoon chili powder, or more to taste
1 teaspoon ground cumin, optional
Freshly ground pepper to taste
Morton Lite Salt® Mixture, to taste, optional

In a heavy, 4-quart Dutch oven sprayed with nonstick spray, stir-fry turkey, onion and garlic over high heat until browned. Drain fat, if any. Stir in remaining ingredients. Simmer, covered, for 2 hours. Stir occasionally.
Serves 10.

Per serving: 296 cal. (36% from fat); 26 g protein; 11.7 g fat (3.1 g sat.); 20.4 g carbo.; 564 mg sodium; 76 mg chol.; 7.7 g fiber. Exchanges: 3 lean meat, 1 bread, 1 vegetable, ½ fat.

Sweet & Sour Turkey Kabobs

Oriental flavor that is sure to please.

1 pound ground turkey breast
1 cup soft bread crumbs
¼ cup nonfat milk
1 can (8 oz.) juice-pack pineapple chunks
¼ cup low-sodium soy sauce
1 teaspoon finely grated fresh ginger (or ½ teaspoon ground ginger)
½ teaspoon each: dry mustard and garlic powder
10 small boiling onions, peeled and microwaved or steamed until barely tender
1 green bell pepper, seeded and cut into 1" chunks
10 cherry tomatoes

In a large bowl, combine turkey, bread crumbs and milk. Mix well and shape into 30 meatballs. Drain pineapple and reserve juice. In a large plastic food bag mix pineapple juice, soy sauce, ginger, mustard and garlic powder. Add meatballs. Seal bag and marinate in refrigerator for several hours or overnight, turning once. Drain meatballs, reserving marinade. Thread meatballs onto 10 skewers, alternating with pineapple, onions and green pepper. Broil 5" from heat for 8 minutes, or until meat is nearly done, turning once and brushing with marinade once. Add tomatoes to the ends of skewers. Broil 2 minutes longer. Serves 5 (2 skewers per serving).

Per serving: 194 cal. (6% from fat); 25 g protein; 1.37 g fat (0.32 g sat.); 20.4 g carbo.; 224 mg sodium; 57 mg chol.; 2.4 g fiber. Exchanges: 3 lean meat, 1 bread, ½ fruit. Add 2 fat exchanges to meal plan.

Pasta & Grains

Linguini with Turkey & Dried Tomatoes

Serve with a green salad and French bread.

¼ cup dried tomatoes packed in oil
2 cloves garlic, minced
2 green onions, thinly sliced
½ each: red and green bell pepper, seeded and cut into thin slices
4 ounces fresh mushrooms, sliced
8 ounces cooked turkey, cut in ¼" by 1½" strips
8 ounces dry linguini, cooked according to package directions, drained and kept warm
1½ teaspoons dried basil
2 packages (1 teaspoon each) chicken bouillon granules
Grated Parmesan cheese, optional

Drain oil from dried tomatoes and discard, except for 2 tablespoons. Cut dried tomatoes into small pieces. In a heavy skillet, stir-fry ⅓ dried tomatoes and 2 teaspoons oil with garlic, green onions and peppers over medium-high heat until crisp-tender. Remove from skillet and keep warm. Add to skillet another ⅓ dried tomatoes and 2 teaspoons oil plus the mushrooms. Stir-fry over medium-high heat until cooked, then remove tomatoes and mushrooms and keep warm with onion-pepper mixture. Next add remaining dried tomatoes and 2 teaspoons oil to skillet, along with the turkey. Stir-fry over medium-high heat until lightly browned. Mix all stir-fried vegetables and turkey with warm, cooked linguini, basil and chicken bouillon granules. Top with grated Parmesan cheese (if used). Serves 6.

Per serving: 237 cal. (22% from fat); 15 g protein; 5.9 g fat (4% sat.); 30.5 g carbo.; 405 mg sodium; 24 mg chol.; 2.64 g fiber. Exchanges: 1 medium-fat meat, 2 bread.

Manicotti Florentine

A satisfying dish for hearty appetites.

½ cup chopped onion
1 large clove garlic, minced
½ package (10 oz.) frozen chopped spinach, drained
1 cup low-fat (1% fat) cottage or ricotta cheese
1 teaspoon dried basil
½ teaspoon dried oregano leaves
½ teaspoon Original Blend Mrs. Dash® seasoning
8 manicotti, cooked according to package directions and drained
1½ cups fat-free spaghetti sauce
½ cup grated fat-free mozzarella cheese

In a skillet sprayed with nonstick spray, stir-fry onion and garlic over medium heat until soft. Add spinach, cottage or ricotta cheese, basil, oregano and Mrs. Dash®. Mix well, then stuff each manicotti with 3 tablespoons of the spinach mixture. Place stuffed manicotti in an 11" by 7" baking dish sprayed with nonstick spray. Pour spaghetti sauce over manicotti. Cover tightly with aluminum foil and bake in a preheated 350° oven for 45 minutes. Uncover, and scatter mozzarella cheese over top. Return to oven for 5 minutes. Serves 4.

Per serving: 231 cal. (5% from fat); 17.6 g protein; 1.25 g fat (0.38 g sat.); 38 g carbo.; 483 mg sodium; 4.4 mg chol.; 5.6 g fiber. Exchanges: 1 lean meat, 2 bread, 1 vegetable.

Fettuccini Alfredo

Pasta with a creamy, rich-tasting sauce.

8 ounces dry fettuccini, cooked according to package directions
1 cup fat-free ranch salad dressing
1 clove garlic, minced
2 green onions, minced
¼ teaspoon hot sauce, optional
½ cup grated Parmesan cheese

Drain hot fettuccini and mix gently with remaining ingredients. Serves 8.

Per serving: 178 cal. (10% from fat); 6.7 g protein; 1.95 g fat (1 g sat.); 22.4 g carbo.; 413 mg sodium; 4 mg chol.; 1 g fiber. Exchanges: 1½ bread.

Quick Macaroni & Cheese

An easy-to-fix family favorite.

1½ cups nonfat milk
2 tablespoons flour
2 packages (1 teaspoon each) chicken bouillon granules
⅛ teaspoon freshly ground pepper
8 ounces dry macaroni or small shell pasta (2 cups), cooked according to package directions, drained and kept warm
2 ounces lean cooked ham, cut into small cubes
8 ounces grated fat-free cheddar cheese
¼ cup chopped green onion

In a blender, mix milk, flour, bouillon granules and pepper. Pour into a large, heavy saucepan. Cook over medium heat, stirring constantly, until thickened. Add pasta, ham, cheese and green onion. Stir gently to mix. Serves 6.

Per serving: 242 cal. (5% from fat); 21.4 g protein; 1.47 g fat (0.37 g sat.); 35 g carbo.; 786 mg sodium; 10.6 mg chol.; 1.48 g fiber. Exchanges: 2 lean meat, ¼ nonfat milk, 2 bread. Add 1 fat exchange to meal plan.

Mushroom-Barley Pilaf

A versatile meal accompaniment.

⅔ cup sliced celery
½ cup chopped onion
1 cup pearl barley, uncooked
2 cups chicken broth
1 cup water
1 can (4 oz.) sliced mushrooms and liquid
1 tablespoon Butter Buds®

In a large, heavy saucepan sprayed with nonstick spray, stir-fry celery and onion over medium-high heat for 3 to 4 minutes, until tender. Add barley, chicken broth, water, mushrooms with liquid and Butter Buds®. Cover tightly and simmer for 1½ hours. (After 1 hour, add ½ cup more water if barley becomes dry.) Serves 6.

Per serving: 125 cal. (8% from fat); 4.8 g protein; 1.06 g fat (0.22 g sat.); 25.3 g carbo.; 440 mg sodium; 0.33 mg chol.; 2.4 g fiber. Exchanges: 1½ bread.

Spaghetti with Clam Sauce

A low-fat version of a favorite Italian dish.

¼ cup minced onion
2 cloves garlic, minced
⅔ cup dry white wine
½ teaspoon Original Blend
  Mrs. Dash® seasoning
1 package (1 teaspoon) chicken
  bouillon granules
2 cans (6.5 oz. each) minced clams,
  drained (reserve juice)
2 tablespoons cornstarch, dissolved
  in clam juice
¼ cup chopped fresh parsley, divided
⅛ teaspoon freshly ground pepper
8 ounces spaghetti, cooked according to
  package directions, drained and kept warm
¼ cup grated Parmesan cheese

In a heavy skillet sprayed with nonstick spray, stir-fry onion and garlic over medium-high heat until soft. Add wine, Mrs. Dash®, chicken bouillon granules, drained clams, dissolved cornstarch, 2 tablespoons parsley and pepper. Simmer over medium heat, stirring constantly, until thickened—about 3 minutes. Pour sauce over hot spaghetti and top with remaining parsley and Parmesan cheese. Serves 6.

Per serving: 225 cal. (9% from fat); 12.2 g protein; 2.2 g fat (0.8 g sat.); 33.5 g carbo.; 651 mg sodium; 18 mg chol.; 1.6 g fiber. Exchanges: 1 lean meat, 2 bread.

Pasta Primavera

Al dente vegetables and lightly seasoned pasta.

8 ounces uncooked fettuccini
1 package (16 oz.) frozen broccoli,
  cauliflower and carrots
1 package (0.4 oz.) fat-free ranch
  salad dressing mix
1 tablespoon olive oil

In a large pot of boiling water, cook fettuccini for 5 minutes over medium heat. Add frozen vegetables and continue to boil until fettuccini is cooked and vegetables are crisp-tender, about 5 minutes longer. Using a colander, drain cooked fettuccini and vegetables, then return to cooking pot. Sprinkle on dry salad dressing mix and add olive oil. Stir gently to mix. Serves 8.

Per serving: 141 cal. (14% from fat); 4.4 g protein; 2.2 g fat (0.3 g sat.); 26 g carbo.; 42 mg sodium; 0 mg chol.; 1.05 g fiber. Exchanges: 1½ bread, ½ vegetable, ½ fat.

Broccoli-Rice Casserole

A delicious accompaniment to roasted or barbecued meats.

2 cups cooked long grain rice
2 packages frozen (10 oz. each) chopped broccoli, steamed until barely tender
1 can (10 oz.) cream of chicken soup
½ cup nonfat milk
1 can sliced water chestnuts, drained and chopped
¼ cup each: chopped celery and onion
1½ cups grated fat-free cheddar cheese (6 oz.), divided

Mix rice, steamed broccoli, soup, milk, chestnuts, celery, onion and 1 cup cheese. Pour into a casserole sprayed with nonstick spray. Top with remaining ½ cup cheese. Bake in a preheated 350° oven for 20 minutes, or until hot. Serves 10.

Per serving: 132 cal. (14% from fat); 9.5 g protein; 2 g fat (0.57 g sat.); 19.3 g carbo.; 384 mg sodium; 5.6 g chol.; 3 g fiber. Exchanges: 1 lean meat, 1 bread.

Chili-Rice-Cheese Casserole

A dish your guests will love!

3 cups cooked long grain rice
1 cup fat-free sour cream
1 can (4 oz.) chili peppers, chopped (discard seeds)
4 ounces fat-free jack or mozzarella cheese, coarsely grated
Paprika

Mix all ingredients together, except paprika. Pour into a large casserole sprayed with nonstick spray and sprinkle top with paprika. Bake in a preheated 350° oven for 35 minutes, or until hot. Serves 6.

Per serving: 169 cal. (1% from fat); 10.6 g protein; 0.21 g fat (0.05 g sat.); 29 g carbo.; 163 mg sodium; 3.3 mg chol.; 0.78 g fiber. Exchanges: ½ lean meat, 2 bread.

East Indian Rice

A delicate blend of exotic flavors.

2¼ cups water
1 cup long grain rice, uncooked
2 packages (1 teaspoon each) chicken bouillon granules
½ teaspoon turmeric or curry powder

In a medium-sized saucepan, bring water to a boil. Add rice, chicken bouillon granules and turmeric or curry powder. Stir to mix. Cover and simmer for 20 minutes. Remove from heat and let stand for 5 minutes. Serves 6.

Per serving: 117 cal. (4% from fat); 2.5 g protein; 0.48 g fat (0.12 g sat.); 25 g carbo.; 373 mg sodium; 0.33 mg chol.; 0.7 g fiber. Exchanges: 1½ bread.

Onion-Rice Pilaf

This is especially delicious with barbecued meats.

1 medium onion, chopped
1 cup long grain rice, uncooked
2 cups water
2 packages (1 teaspoon each) chicken bouillon granules
⅛ teaspoon pepper
2 tablespoons chopped fresh parsley

Heat a large, heavy skillet sprayed with nonstick spray over medium-high heat. Add onion and stir-fry until tender. Add rice. Cook and stir until lightly browned. Add water, chicken bouillon granules and pepper. Bring to a boil, then cover and simmer for 20 minutes. Stir in parsley. Serves 6.

Per serving: 124 cal. (4% from fat); 2.75 g protein; 0.49 g fat (0 g sat.); 26.5 g carbo.; 375 mg sodium; 0.33 mg chol.; 1 g fiber. Exchanges: 1½ bread.

Couscous with Pine Nuts

Serve with poultry, fish or meat.

¼ cup each: chopped onion, celery and parsley
2⅓ cups water
2 packages (1 teaspoon each) chicken bouillon granules
10 ounces couscous, uncooked
3 tablespoons toasted pine nuts*
3 tablespoons raisins, optional

Heat a heavy saucepan over medium-high heat, then spray with nonstick spray. Add celery and onion, stir-frying until lightly browned. Add water, chicken bouillon granules and parsley. Heat to boiling, then stir in couscous. Cover and remove from heat. Let stand 5 minutes. Fluff couscous lightly with a fork, then spoon into a large serving bowl. Top with pine nuts and raisins (if used). Serves 10.

*To toast, bake at 300° on an ungreased baking sheet until golden.

Per serving: 122 cal. (17% from fat); 4.8 g protein; 2.3 g fat (0.37 g sat.); 21.3 g carbo.; 229 mg sodium; 0.2 mg chol.; 0.15 g fiber. Exchanges: 1½ bread, ½ fat.

Vegetables

Asparagus with Parmesan Cheese

Asparagus in a buttery cheese-garlic sauce.

1 pound asparagus
1 clove garlic, minced
1 package (3 tablespoons) Butter Buds®
1 package (1 teaspoon) chicken bouillon granules
¼ cup water
¼ cup grated Parmesan cheese

Peel stems of asparagus with a vegetable peeler, then cut off any remaining tough ends. Place asparagus in a large skillet with garlic, Butter Buds®, chicken bouillon granules and water. Cover; simmer asparagus for 3 to 5 minutes, or until just tender. Turn asparagus over gently to coat in garlic-butter sauce in skillet. Sprinkle each serving with Parmesan cheese. Serves 4.

Per serving: 72 cal. (30% from fat); 6 g protein; 2.4 g fat (1.2 g sat.); 10 g carbo.; 390 mg sodium; 4.5 mg chol.; 1.2 g fiber. Exchanges: 2 vegetable, ½ fat.

Creole Green Beans

Green beans with a light, savory seasoning.

1 pound green beans, with ends and strings removed, cut into 2" pieces
1 small onion, chopped
1 large clove garlic, minced
¼ cup minced celery
1 tomato, chopped
½ cup water
1 package (1 teaspoon) chicken bouillon granules
Dash freshly ground pepper

In a covered saucepan, cook all ingredients over medium heat, stirring occasionally, until tender—about 20 minutes. Serves 8.

Per serving: 20 cal. (11% from fat); 1.13 g protein; 0.25 g fat (0.05 g sat.); 4.3 g carbo.; 499 mg sodium; 0.13 mg chol.; 2.26 g fiber. Exchanges: Free for one serving.

Stir-Fried Corn with Peppers

A colorful, flavorful vegetable combination.

½ each: red and green bell pepper, seeded and diced
2 cups fresh corn kernels
1½ packages (1½ teaspoons total) chicken bouillon granules

In a large, heavy skillet sprayed with nonstick spray, stir-fry peppers over medium-high heat for 3 minutes. Add corn and chicken bouillon granules. Reduce heat to medium and cover. Cook for 5 minutes longer, stirring occasionally, until corn is hot. Serves 6.

Per serving: 66 cal. (14% from fat); 2.15 g protein; 1 g fat (0.19 g sat.); 14.7 g carbo.; 288 mg sodium; 0.25 mg chol.; 3.4 g fiber. Exchanges: 1 bread.

Sweet & Sour Red Cabbage

A delicious blend of sweet & sour flavors.

1 onion, chopped
4 cups thinly sliced red cabbage
1 large Golden Delicious apple, peeled, cored and thinly sliced
⅓ cup water
1 teaspoon Morton Lite Salt® Mixture
⅛ teaspoon freshly ground pepper
¼ cup wine vinegar
  Sugar substitute equal to 2 tablespoons brown sugar (i.e., 2 tablespoons Brown SugarTwin®), or more to taste

In a large, heavy skillet sprayed with nonstick spray, stir-fry onion over medium heat until soft. Add cabbage, apple, water, Morton Lite Salt® Mixture and pepper. Cover; simmer, stirring occasionally, for 20 minutes, or until cabbage is tender. (If mixture becomes too dry, add a little more water.) Remove from heat and stir in vinegar and sugar substitute. Serves 4.

Per serving: 45 cal. (6% from fat); 1.26 g protein; 0.32 g fat (0.04 g sat.); 10.8 g carbo.; 297 mg sodium; 0 mg chol.; 4.6 g fiber. Exchanges: ⅔ fruit.

Chinese-Style Broccoli

Crisp-tender broccoli in an oriental sauce.

3 cups broccoli florets
½ cup water
1½ tablespoons low-sodium soy sauce
½ tablespoon sesame oil
1 teaspoon toasted sesame seeds*

Cook broccoli with water in a covered saucepan over medium heat for 5 to 7 minutes, until crisp-tender. Drain well. Mix soy sauce with sesame oil. Pour over broccoli and toss gently to mix. Top with toasted sesame seeds. Serves 6.

*To toast, stir in a dry heavy skillet over medium heat until golden, about 5 minutes.

Per serving: 28 cal. (49% from fat); 1.8 g protein; 1.53 g fat (0.22 g sat.); 2.7 g carbo.; 31 mg sodium; 0 mg chol.; 0.5 g fiber. Exchanges: 1 vegetable.

Carrots & Zucchini with Basil

This colorful stir-fry is quick to fix.

2 medium carrots, peeled
2 medium zucchini
1 tablespoon olive oil
1 large green onion, minced
2 cloves garlic, minced
1 package (1 teaspoon) chicken bouillon granules
1 teaspoon fresh basil leaves, chopped (or ½ teaspoon dried basil)
Freshly ground pepper to taste

Cut carrots and zucchini into julienne strips the size of wooden matchsticks. In a large, heavy skillet, stir-fry carrots in oil over medium-high heat until they begin to soften. Add zucchini and continue to stir-fry for 2 minutes more. Add green onion and garlic. Cook 1 minute longer, stirring often. Remove from heat and add chicken bouillon granules, basil and fresh pepper. Serves 4.

Per serving: 58 cal. (57% from fat); 1.14 g protein; 3.7 g fat (0.5 g sat.); 5.6 g carbo.; 205 mg sodium; 0 mg chol.; 2.35 g fiber. Exchanges: 1 vegetable, ½ fat.

Gingered Carrots

Ginger and orange juice lend a slightly sweet and spicy flavor.

1 pound carrots, peeled and cut into ¼" diagonal slices
¼ cup water
1 package (1 teaspoon) chicken bouillon granules
1 teaspoon finely grated fresh ginger
1 tablespoon orange juice concentrate, optional
Sugar substitute equal to ½ teaspoon sugar (i.e., ½ teaspoon SugarTwin®)
1 tablespoon chopped fresh parsley

Cook carrots with water and chicken bouillon granules in a heavy, covered saucepan over medium-high heat until barely tender—about 5 minutes. Cooking liquid should nearly disappear. Add ginger, orange juice concentrate (if used) and sugar substitute. Stir well. Garnish with parsley. Serves 4.

Per serving: 43 cal. (9% from fat); 1.33 g protein; 0.42 g fat (0.09 g sat.); 9.2 g carbo.; 337 mg sodium; 0.25 mg chol.; 3.9 g fiber. Exchanges: ½ bread or 2 vegetable.

Eggplant Parmigiana

A "slimmed-down" version of an Italian favorite.

½ pound very lean ground beef
1 clove garlic, minced
1 cup fat-free spaghetti sauce
1 teaspoon Original Blend
   Mrs. Dash® seasoning
1 medium eggplant, peeled and cut into
   ½" thick slices
¼ cup grated Parmesan cheese, divided

In a large skillet sprayed with nonstick spray, brown beef and garlic. Mix in spaghetti sauce and Mrs. Dash®. Spread ½ of the eggplant slices in the bottom of an 8" by 12" baking pan sprayed with nonstick spray. Cover with half of the beef-spaghetti sauce mixture. Sprinkle with 2 tablespoons Parmesan cheese. Repeat with another layer of eggplant. Cover with the remaining beef-spaghetti sauce. Top with remaining Parmesan cheese. Cover tightly with lid or aluminum foil and bake in a preheated 350° oven for 50 to 60 minutes, or until eggplant is tender. Serves 4.

Per serving: 148 cal. (50% from fat); 10.6 g protein; 8.3 g fat (3.7 g sat.); 6.8 g carbo.; 315 mg sodium; 31 mg chol.; 1.26 g fiber. Exchanges: 1 high-fat meat, 1 vegetable.

Eggplant Au Gratin

This is a light, soufflé-like dish that is easy to prepare!

1 large eggplant, peeled and cut into
   pieces
1 medium onion, peeled and cut
   into pieces
½ cup water
1 slice white bread, crumbled in blender
⅔ cup grated fat-free cheddar cheese,
   divided
1 egg, beaten
¼ teaspoon Morton Lite Salt® Mixture
½ teaspoon Original Blend
   Mrs. Dash® seasoning

Simmer eggplant and onion with water in a tightly covered saucepan until tender. Drain well. When cool, chop into small pieces. Add bread, ⅓ cup cheese, egg, Morton Lite Salt® Mixture and Mrs. Dash®. Pour into a large loaf pan sprayed with nonstick spray and top with remaining cheese. Bake in a preheated 350° oven for 20 minutes. Serves 6.

Per serving: 56 cal. (16% from fat); 6.3 g protein; 1 g fat (0.3 g sat.); 5.6 g carbo.; 185 mg sodium; 38 mg chol.; 0.6 g fiber. Exchanges: ½ lean meat, 1 vegetable.

Creamy Mashed Potatoes

A traditional family favorite.

5 medium potatoes (2½ lbs.), peeled and cut into quarters
1 teaspoon each: Morton Lite Salt® Mixture, dried parsley flakes and dried onion flakes
1 package (3 tablespoons) Butter Buds®
½ cup nonfat milk powder
¼ teaspoon freshly ground pepper
½ teaspoon garlic powder

Place peeled potatoes in a large pot and cover with water. Cover; simmer for 30 minutes, or until potatoes are tender. Drain, but reserve cooking liquid. Mash potatoes with a potato masher. Add ½ cup hot reserved cooking liquid and remaining ingredients. Mash until well blended. Serves 8.

Per serving: 87 cal. (1% from fat); 4.1 g protein; 0.12 g fat (0.06 g sat.); 18.2 g carbo.; 251 mg sodium; 1.5 mg chol.; 0.31 g fiber. Exchanges: 1 bread.

Oven French Fries

Crisp, tasty and fat-free!

3 medium baking potatoes, unpeeled, cut into french fry-sized pieces
⅓ teaspoon Morton Lite Salt® Mixture

Arrange potato pieces in a single layer on a large metal baking sheet sprayed with nonstick spray. Spray potato pieces with nonstick spray. Bake in a preheated 475° oven until golden, about 20 minutes, turning occasionally. During cooking, remove potato pieces that are golden, and allow others to cook longer. Sprinkle with Morton Lite Salt® Mixture. Serves 3.

Per serving: 110 cal. (1% from fat); 3.3 g protein; 0.15 g fat (0.04 g sat.); 25 g carbo.; 155 mg sodium; 0 mg chol.; 2.8 g fiber. Exchanges: 1½ bread.

Scalloped Potatoes

A rich-tasting dish that's sure to please.

3 large potatoes, peeled and sliced
¼ cup finely chopped onion
2 tablespoons flour
1¼ cups nonfat milk, heated
1 package (3 tablespoons) Butter Buds®
1 teaspoon Morton Lite Salt® Mixture
¼ teaspoon each: paprika and dry mustard

Layer potatoes and onion in a 10" baking dish sprayed with nonstick spray, sprinkling each layer with flour. Mix milk with Butter Buds® and seasonings, and pour over potatoes. Bake in a preheated 350° oven for 1½ hours. Cover with aluminum foil if the potatoes start to become dry. Serves 6.

Per serving: 81 cal. (7% from fat); 3.1 g protein; 0.62 g fat (0.35 g sat.); 17 g carbo.; 305 mg sodium; 2.1 mg chol.; 0.38 g fiber. Exchanges: 1 bread.

Creamed Spinach

Spinach in a well-seasoned, creamy sauce.

1 package (10 oz.) frozen chopped spinach
½ cup nonfat milk powder
1 cup water
1 package (1 teaspoon) chicken bouillon granules
2 tablespoons flour
Freshly ground pepper to taste

Cook spinach according to package directions; drain well and keep warm. In a blender, mix remaining ingredients. Pour into a saucepan and cook over medium heat, stirring constantly, until thickened. Add cooked spinach and stir to mix. Serves 4.

Per serving: 77 cal. (8% from fat); 6.9 g protein; 0.69 g fat (0.24 g sat.); 11.9 g carbo.; 377 mg sodium; 2.25 mg chol.; 3.1 g fiber. Exchanges: 1 vegetable, ⅓ bread, ¼ nonfat milk.

Spinach with Sesame Seeds

Stir-fried spinach with oriental seasonings.

1½ tablespoons sesame seeds
1 tablespoon sesame oil
3 large cloves garlic, minced
1½ pounds fresh spinach, washed and trimmed of stems
2 teaspoons low-sodium soy sauce
1 tablespoon rice vinegar

Toast sesame seeds in dry heavy skillet over medium heat, stirring constantly, until golden. Remove from skillet when lightly browned. Add oil and garlic to skillet and cook over medium heat for 4 minutes, or until soft. Add spinach. Stir-fry over medium-high heat until spinach is wilted and most of liquid has evaporated, about 4 minutes. Remove cooked spinach to a serving platter. Sprinkle with sesame seeds, soy sauce and rice vinegar. Serves 4.

Per serving: 85 cal. (59% from fat); 4.6 g protein; 5.6 g fat (0.6 g sat.); 7.4 g carbo; 171 mg sodium; 0 mg chol.; 7 g fiber. Exchanges: 1 vegetable, 1 fat.

Tomatoes Provençale

A delicious and colorful meal accompaniment.

6 fresh, ripe medium tomatoes
1 slice French bread, crumbled
   in a blender
¼ cup grated Parmesan cheese
   Dash freshly ground pepper
2 cloves garlic, finely minced
2 tablespoons each: Butter Buds®
   and chopped fresh parsley

Wash and core, but do not peel, tomatoes. Cut them in half crosswise and place cut side up on a shallow baking sheet sprayed with nonstick spray. Mix bread crumbs, cheese, pepper, garlic, Butter Buds® and parsley. Top each tomato half with an equal amount of the bread mixture. Bake in a preheated 450° oven for 10 minutes. Serves 6.

Per serving: 51 cal. (26% from fat); 2.8 g protein; 1.47 g fat (0.71 g sat.); 7.6 g carbo.; 96 mg sodium; 2.67 mg chol.; 1.5 g fiber. Exchanges: 1 vegetable.

Tomatoes & Okra

A succulent blend of tempting flavors.

1½ cups fresh okra, with ends removed,
   cut into ½" slices
½ cup water
¼ cup each: chopped onion and chopped,
   seeded bell pepper
3 medium tomatoes, peeled and cut
   into pieces
1 package (1 teaspoon) chicken
   bouillon granules
¼ teaspoon freshly ground pepper
   Sugar substitute equal to 1 tablespoon
   sugar (i.e., 1 tablespoon SugarTwin®)
1 teaspoon cornstarch, dissolved in
   2 tablespoons water

In a covered saucepan, cook okra in ½ cup boiling water for 10 minutes. Drain, and discard liquid. In a heavy skillet sprayed with nonstick spray, cook onion and pepper over medium heat until tender but not brown. Add cooked okra, tomatoes, chicken bouillon granules, pepper, sugar substitute and dissolved cornstarch. Cook until heated through, stirring often. Serves 4.

Per serving: 107 cal. (10% from fat); 5.7 g protein; 1.18 g fat (1 g sat.); 24 g carbo.; 211 mg sodium; 0 mg chol.; 6.2 g fiber. Exchanges: 1 bread, 1 vegetable.

Easy Stuffed Zucchini

A quick-to-fix au gratin dish.

2 medium zucchini, with ends removed, cut in half lengthwise
¼ cup fat-free spaghetti sauce or tomato sauce
1 large clove garlic, minced
¼ teaspoon Morton Lite Salt® Mixture
1 teaspoon Original Blend Mrs. Dash® seasoning
½ cup cooked rice
½ cup grated fat-free cheddar cheese

Place zucchini in a large skillet, cut side down. Add ½ cup water, cover, and cook over medium heat until barely tender—about 8 minutes. Remove and let cool slightly. Using a spoon, scoop out center part of each zucchini half, leaving about ½" shell. Cut scooped-out zucchini into ½" pieces. Place in a large strainer and squeeze out excess liquid. In a bowl, mix zucchini with spaghetti sauce or tomato sauce, garlic, Morton Lite Salt® Mixture, Mrs. Dash®, rice and grated cheese. Spoon this mixture into zucchini halves and place them in a baking dish. Bake for about 20 minutes in a preheated 350° oven, or until heated through. Serves 4.

Per serving: 69 cal. (2% from fat); 6.2 g protein; 0.17 g fat (0.03 g sat.); 10.7 g carbo.; 223 mg sodium; 2.5 mg chol.; 2.42 g fiber. Exchanges: ½ bread, 1 vegetable.

Zucchini with Mushrooms

A versatile, gourmet side dish.

½ medium onion, chopped
1 clove garlic, minced
8 ounces mushrooms, washed and thinly sliced
4 medium (about 2 lbs.) zucchini, grated
2 eggs, beaten
½ teaspoon each: dried oregano leaves and Morton Lite Salt® Mixture
1 teaspoon Original Blend Mrs. Dash® seasoning
3 tablespoons grated Parmesan cheese

In a heavy skillet sprayed with nonstick spray, stir-fry onion and garlic over medium-high heat until golden brown. Transfer from skillet to a mixing bowl. Respray skillet and stir-fry mushrooms until golden brown. Add to browned onion and garlic. Add zucchini, eggs, oregano, Morton Lite Salt® Mixture and Mrs. Dash®. Mix well, then pour into a shallow 9" by 12" casserole sprayed with nonstick spray. Bake in a preheated 325° oven for 45 minutes, or until set. Top with grated cheese. Serves 8.

Per serving: 41 cal. (40% from fat); 3.2 g protein; 1.8 g fat (0.65 g sat.); 3.6 g carbo.; 115 mg sodium; 54 mg chol.; 2.5 g fiber. Exchanges: 1 vegetable.

Grilled Vegetable Kabobs

A colorful blend of flavors and textures.

½ cup fat-free Italian salad dressing
1 tablespoon minced fresh parsley or
   1 teaspoon dried parsley flakes
1 teaspoon dried basil
1 medium zucchini, cut into 1" slices
1 medium yellow squash, cut into 1" slices
8 small boiling onions, peeled and
   microwaved until barely tender
8 medium mushrooms
8 cherry tomatoes

Combine all ingredients in a large plastic food bag. Seal and refrigerate for several hours. Alternate zucchini, squash, onions and mushrooms on 8 skewers. Barbecue 4" above hot coals for 10 minutes; baste with remaining marinade and turn frequently. Add tomatoes to skewer ends and continue to barbecue for 5 minutes longer. Serves 4.

Per serving: 55 cal. (8% from fat); 2.6 g protein; 0.48 g fat (0.06 g sat.); 12.2 g carbo.; 303 mg sodium; 0 mg chol.; 4.3 g fiber. Exchanges: 1 bread or 2 vegetable.

Oven-Roasted Vegetables

Flavorful and easy to prepare.

4 small red potatoes, scrubbed and
   cut in half
4 small carrots, peeled and cut into
   1" chunks
4 small zucchini, with ends removed,
   cut into 1" chunks
1 red or green bell pepper, seeded and
   cut into 8 pieces
8 mushrooms
1 teaspoon each: Morton Lite Salt®
   Mixture and Original Blend
   Mrs. Dash® seasoning

Spray a large, heavy skillet with nonstick spray. Add potatoes and carrots. Spray vegetables in skillet with nonstick spray, then sprinkle with part of the Morton Lite Salt® Mixture and Mrs. Dash®. Cover tightly with aluminum foil and roast in a preheated 400° oven for 25 minutes. Remove skillet from oven and add zucchini, pepper and mushrooms. Spray vegetables with nonstick spray and sprinkle with remaining salt and seasoning. Return to 400° oven and roast, uncovered, 15 to 20 minutes longer. Serves 4.

Per serving: 78 cal. (5% from fat); 3.1 g protein; 0.43 g fat (0.07 g fat); 17 g carbo.; 308 mg sodium; 0 mg chol.; 4.3 g fiber. Exchanges: 1 bread.

Sauces & Marinades

Creamy Parmesan Sauce

Serve with cooked, cubed poultry and plain rice or pasta.

1 cup low-fat (1% fat) milk
⅓ cup white wine (or substitute ⅓ cup low-fat milk)
1 package (1 teaspoon) chicken bouillon granules
¼ cup grated Parmesan cheese
3 tablespoons flour

Mix all ingredients in a blender. Pour into a heavy saucepan and cook, stirring constantly, over medium heat until thickened. Makes 1½ cups. Serves 6 (¼ cup per serving).

Per serving: 60 cal. (24% from fat); 3 g protein; 1.6 g fat (1 g sat.); 5 g carbo.; 269 mg sodium; 4.5 mg chol.; 0.1 g fiber. Exchanges: ½ bread.

Hickory Barbecue Sauce

Adds spicy flavor to barbecued meats.

½ cup catsup
¼ cup red wine
1 tablespoon Worcestershire sauce
1 clove garlic, minced
½ teaspoon hot pepper sauce
½ teaspoon hickory-flavored salt
Sugar substitute equal to 2 tablespoons brown sugar (i.e., 2 tablespoons Brown SugarTwin®)

In a covered saucepan, simmer catsup, wine, Worcestershire sauce, garlic, hot pepper sauce and hickory-flavored salt for 10 minutes. Remove from heat and stir in sugar substitute. Use to baste chicken, pork or beef during the last 20 minutes of barbecuing. Refrigerate for up to 2 weeks. Serves 6 (2 tablespoons per serving).

Per serving: 30 cal. (4% from fat); 0.47 g protein; 0.13 g fat (0.01 g sat.); 5.7 g carbo.; 329 mg sodium; 0 mg chol.; 0.13 g fiber. Exchanges: ⅓ bread.

Quick Cheese Sauce

Delicious with a medley of steamed broccoli, cauliflower and carrots.

¾ cup grated fat-free cheddar cheese (3 oz.)
¼ cup fat-free ranch salad dressing
1 package (1 teaspoon) chicken bouillon granules
½ cup water

Mix all ingredients in a large, heat-proof glass measuring cup. Heat in a microwave oven, stirring occasionally, until melted. Serves 4 (⅓ cup per person).

Per serving: 59 cal. (3% from fat); 7.5 g protein; 0.21 g fat (0.05 g sat.); 1.52 g carbo.; 584 mg sodium; 4 mg chol.; 0 g fiber. Exchanges: 1 lean meat. Add ½ fat exchange to meal plan.

Lite Pesto Sauce

A versatile sauce for pasta.

2 cups fresh basil leaves
2 large cloves garlic, minced
½ cup fresh parsley
⅓ cup chicken broth
½ cup grated Parmesan cheese
2 tablespoons olive oil
¼ teaspoon each: Morton Lite Salt®
　Mixture and pepper
1 tablespoon Butter Buds®

In a food processor or blender, mix all ingredients until smooth. Refrigerate for up to 2 days, or freeze for longer storage. Serves 8 (2 tablespoons per serving).

Per serving: 64 cal. (73% from fat); 3.25 g protein; 5.2 g fat (1.48 g sat.); 1.95 g carbo.; 227 mg sodium; 4.1 mg chol.; 0.83 g fiber. Exchanges: ½ high-fat meat.

Easy Hollandaise Sauce

A rich-tasting sauce, perfect for steamed vegetables.

6 tablespoons fat-free mayonnaise
2 teaspoons Dijon mustard
2 tablespoons rice vinegar
3 tablespoons water
　Sugar substitute equal to 1 tablespoon
　sugar (i. e., 1½ packets Equal®)

Mix all ingredients together. Refrigerate for up to 2 weeks. Serves 4 (3 tablespoons per serving).

Per serving: 18 cal. (5% from fat); 0.1 g protein; 0.1 g fat (0 g sat.); 3.65 g carbo.; 182 mg sodium; 0 mg chol.; 0 g fiber. Exchanges: Free for 1 serving.

Teriyaki Sauce

Delicious as a marinade or as a dipping sauce.

1 cup low-sodium soy sauce
¼ cup grated onion
¼ cup dry sherry
1 clove garlic, minced
1 teaspoon finely grated fresh ginger or
　½ teaspoon dried ground ginger
2 tablespoons lemon juice
　Sugar substitute equal to 1 tablespoon
　brown sugar (i. e., 1 tablespoon Brown
　SugarTwin®)

Mix all ingredients together. Refrigerate for up to 1 week. Serves 8 (3 tablespoons per serving).

Per serving: 30 cal. (0% from fat); 3 g protein; 0.01 g fat (0 g sat.); 3.5 g carbo.; 151 mg sodium; 0 mg chol.; 0.18 g fiber. Exchanges: 1 vegetable.

Sweet & Sour Sauce

For a quick meal, serve this sauce with leftover cooked pork or poultry.

¼ cup rice vinegar
⅔ cup unsweetened pineapple juice
2 tablespoons low-sodium soy sauce
1 package (1 teaspoon) chicken bouillon granules
¼ cup chopped onion
½ each: red and green bell pepper, seeded and cut into ½" cubes
1½ tablespoons cornstarch, dissolved in ½ cup water
1 cup juice-pack pineapple tidbits
Sugar substitute equal to ¼ cup sugar (i.e., 6 packets Equal®), or more to taste

In a saucepan, combine vinegar, pineapple juice, soy sauce, chicken bouillon granules, onion and bell pepper. Simmer for 4 minutes, until vegetables are hot but still crisp. Add dissolved cornstarch and cook until thickened, stirring constantly. Remove from heat and stir in pineapple and sugar substitute. Serves 6 (½ cup per serving).

Per serving: 62 cal. (3% from fat); 1.06 g protein; 0.24 g fat (0.04 g sat.); 14.4 g carbo.; 212 mg sodium; 0.16 mg chol.; 0.64 g fiber. Exchanges: 1 fruit.

Lite Curry Sauce

Serve with cubed leftover chicken or turkey breast and Apricot Chutney (see p. 120).

1 small apple, cored and chopped
1 small onion, chopped
½ teaspoon finely grated fresh ginger or ¼ teaspoon dried ground ginger
1 tablespoon curry powder
2 cups low-fat (1% fat) milk
Dash of red pepper sauce
2 packages (1 teaspoon each) chicken bouillon granules
2 tablespoons flour
1 tablespoon lemon juice
½ teaspoon grated lemon peel
Sugar substitute equal to 2 tablespoons sugar (i.e., 2 tablespoons SugarTwin®)
2 tablespoons raisins
⅓ cup shredded dried coconut

In a skillet sprayed with nonstick spray, stir-fry apple, onion, ginger and curry powder over medium heat until tender. In a blender or food processor, blend cooked apple-onion mixture and remaining ingredients until smooth. Pour into a medium-sized saucepan, cover and simmer for 30 minutes. Serves 8 (¼ cup per serving).

Per serving: 71 cal. (29% from fat); 2.74 g protein; 2.3 g fat (1.67 g sat.); 10.4 g carbo.; 321 mg sodium; 2.75 mg chol.; 0.54 g fiber. Exchanges: ¼ low-fat milk, ½ fruit.

Mushroom Sauce

A creamy, rich-tasting sauce.

2 cups sliced fresh mushrooms
1 clove garlic, minced
2 tablespoons flour
1 cup nonfat milk
⅛ teaspoon pepper
1 package (1 teaspoon) chicken bouillon granules
2 tablespoons chopped fresh parsley
2 tablespoons grated Parmesan cheese

In a heavy saucepan sprayed with nonstick spray, stir-fry mushrooms and garlic over medium-high heat until golden. Mix flour, milk, pepper and bouillon granules in a blender. Pour into saucepan with cooked mushrooms and garlic. Cook over medium heat, stirring constantly, until thickened. Stir in parsley and Parmesan cheese. Serves 4 (⅓ cup per serving).

Per serving: 61 cal. (19% from fat); 4.6 g protein; 1.26 g fat (0.63 g sat.); 8.3 g carbo.; 359 mg sodium; 3.25 mg chol.; 1.07 g fiber. Exchanges: 1 vegetable, ¼ nonfat milk.

Marinara Sauce

Serve with your favorite pasta.

1 medium onion, chopped
2 large cloves garlic, minced
1 28 oz. can (3½ cups) canned tomatoes with juice
¼ cup chopped fresh parsley
½ teaspoon each: dried basil, oregano and Morton Lite Salt® Mixture
¼ teaspoon freshly ground pepper
⅛ teaspoon hot pepper flakes, optional

In a large saucepan sprayed with nonstick spray, stir-fry onions and garlic over medium heat until soft. Add remaining ingredients and simmer uncovered for 1 hour, or until sauce is thickened. Makes 6 servings (⅓ cup per serving).

Per serving: 41 cal. (9% from fat); 1.7 g protein; 0.42 g fat (0.06 g sat.); 9 g carbo.; 374 mg sodium; 0 mg chol.; 1.77 g fiber. Exchanges: ½ bread.

Tartar Sauce

This is delicious served with fish.

½ cup fat-free ranch salad dressing
2 tablespoons each: minced celery, green onion and dill pickle

Mix all ingredients together. Refrigerate for up to 1 week. Serves 4 (3 tablespoons per serving).

Per serving: 52 cal. (0% from fat); 1 g protein; 0.01 g fat (0 g sat.); 11.3 g carbo.; 319 mg sodium; 0 mg chol.; 0.08 g fiber. Exchanges: ⅔ bread.

Sour Cream Topping

This is great on baked potatoes.

½ cup fat-free sour cream
½ teaspoon each: garlic salt and onion powder
1 teaspoon Original Blend Mrs. Dash® seasoning
2 teaspoons dried parsley flakes

Mix all ingredients together. Refrigerate for up to 2 weeks. Serves 4 (2 tablespoons per serving).

Per serving: 21 cal. (0% from fat); 2 g protein; 0 g fat (0 g sat.); 3.1 g carbo.; 276 mg sodium; 0 mg chol.; 0 g fiber. Exchanges: Free for 1 serving.

Cranberry Sauce

Serve with the traditional Thanksgiving dinner.

1 package (12 oz.) cranberries, fresh or frozen
1 cup water
Sugar substitute equal to 1½ cups sugar (i.e., 36 packets Equal®)

In a saucepan, simmer cranberries with water over medium heat for 10 minutes, until skins begin to pop. Remove from heat. Stir in sugar substitute. Serve chilled. Makes 15 servings (2 tablespoons per serving).

Per serving: 17 cal. (2% from fat); 0.06 g protein; 0.03 g fat (0 g sat.); 4.3 g carbo.; 0.17 mg sodium; 0 mg chol.; 1.38 g fiber. Exchanges: Free for 1 serving..

Cinnamon Applesauce

Delicious as a dessert or a meal accompaniment.

6 medium Golden Delicious apples (about 1½ pounds)
⅔ cup water
½ teaspoon ground cinnamon
1 tablespoon lemon juice
Sugar substitute equal to ½ cup sugar (i.e., 12 packets Equal®)

Wash apples. Cut into quarters and remove cores. Cut each apple quarter into 6 pieces. Simmer apples with water and cinnamon in a covered saucepan for 30 minutes, until skins are tender. Remove from heat and add lemon juice and sugar substitute. Put through a strainer or whirl in a blender if a smooth applesauce is desired. Serves 8 (½ cup per serving).

Per serving: 66 cal. (5% from fat); 0.22 g protein; 0.37 g fat (0.07 g sat.); 17 g carbo.; 0.75 mg sodium; 0 mg chol.; 2.4 g fiber. Exchanges: 1 fruit.

Breakfast & Brunch

Eggs Benedict

A very special brunch treat!

1 tablespoon flour
½ cup water
½ teaspoon chicken bouillon granules
1 egg yolk
1 teaspoon lemon juice
3 slices (1 oz. each) cooked lean ham, warmed in microwave oven
3 eggs, poached and kept warm
1½ English muffins, toasted
  Freshly ground pepper to taste
1 teaspoon chopped parsley

Mix flour, water, chicken bouillon granules, egg yolk and lemon juice in blender. Pour into a small, heavy saucepan and cook over medium heat, stirring constantly, until thickened. Place one ham slice on top of each toasted muffin half. Top with poached egg. Pour an equal amount of hot sauce over each egg. Grind fresh pepper over top and garnish with chopped parsley. Serves 3.

Per serving: 250 cal. (36% from fat); 21 g protein; 10 g fat (3.1 g sat.); 17.4 g carbo.; 860 mg sodium; 299 mg chol.; 0.22 g fiber. Exchanges: 3 lean meat, 1 bread.

Denver Omelet

Full of flavor, yet low in calories.

½ cup cooked lean ham, diced
¼ cup each: chopped onion and green bell pepper
2 eggs
4 egg whites
  Dash Morton Lite Salt® Mixture

Heat a heavy skillet over medium-high heat, then spray with nonstick spray. Add ham, onion and green pepper. Stir-fry until vegetables are tender. Mix eggs and egg whites with Morton Lite Salt® Mixture. Spray a 7" skillet with nonstick spray and heat over medium heat. Pour in ½ of beaten eggs and sprinkle with ½ of cooked ham-onion-pepper mixture. Let eggs cook for about 8 seconds. Swirl skillet as eggs begin to set, lifting sides with a spatula to allow uncooked egg to run underneath. When omelet is set, gently slide it onto a warm plate, rolling it over so seam side is down. Repeat process with the remaining eggs and ham mixture. Serves 2.

Per serving: 158 cal. (37% from fat); 19.6 g protein; 6.5 g fat (2 g sat.); 3.7 g carbo.; 533 mg sodium; 221 mg chol.; 0.59 g fiber. Exchanges: 2 lean meat, 1 vegetable.

Joe's Special Omelet

A gourmet treat—delicious anytime!

½ pound low-fat turkey sausage, cut into small pieces
1 medium onion, chopped
1 clove garlic, minced
1 cup sliced mushrooms
½ teaspoon Morton Lite Salt® Mixture
⅛ teaspoon freshly ground pepper
2 cups fresh spinach leaves
2 eggs
2 egg whites
¼ cup grated Parmesan cheese

In a large, heavy skillet sprayed with nonstick spray, stir-fry sausage, onion and garlic over medium-high heat until browned. Drain fat, if any. Add mushrooms, Morton Lite Salt® Mixture and pepper. Continue stir-frying over medium-high heat for 2 minutes. Add spinach and cook 1 minute longer. Beat eggs and egg whites together. Pour over sausage-vegetable mixture in skillet. Again cook 1 minute longer, stirring frequently. Remove from heat and top with grated cheese. Serves 4.

Per serving: 225 cal. (45% from fat); 23 g protein; 11.3 g fat (3.66 g sat.); 7 g carbo.; 422 mg sodium; 158 mg chol.; 3.65 g fiber. Exchanges: 3 lean meat, 1 vegetable.

Italian Omelet

Colorful, flavorful and satisfying.

½ each: red and green bell pepper, seeded and diced
2 green onions, sliced
½ cup cooked lean ham, diced
1 small red potato, cooked until tender and cut into ½" cubes
2 eggs
2 egg whites
   Dash freshly ground pepper
2 tablespoons chopped fresh parsley
3 tablespoons grated Parmesan cheese, optional

In a heavy skillet sprayed with nonstick spray, stir-fry bell pepper and onion over medium-high heat until soft. Add ham and cubed potato and heat through, stirring often. Beat eggs and egg whites with pepper until blended and pour over mixture in skillet. Do not stir. Cover and cook on low leat until eggs are set, about 2 minutes. Top with chopped parsley and Parmesan cheese. Serves 2.

Per serving: 169 cal. (35% from fat); 16.7 g protein; 6.6 g fat (2 g sat.); 9.8 g carbo.; 442 mg sodium; 221 mg chol.; 1 g fiber. Exchanges: 2 lean meat, ⅓ bread, 1 vegetable.

Perfect Omelet

Serve this omelet with your choice of the fillings below.

2 eggs
4 egg whites
1/16 teaspoon Morton Lite Salt® Mixture
1 tablespoon water
Dash pepper
2 parsley sprigs

Beat eggs, egg whites, Morton Lite Salt® Mixture, water and pepper with a fork until thoroughly blended. Heat a heavy omelet pan over medium heat, then spray with nonstick spray. Pour in ½ of beaten eggs. Let eggs cook for 8 seconds. Swirl pan as eggs begin to set, lifting around the edges with a spatula to allow uncooked egg to run underneath. The omelet is done when the egg no longer runs freely but the top still looks creamy. Spoon ½ of the filling (see recipes below) across the center of the omelet, and then fold omelet over. Slide onto a warm serving dish. Garnish with parsley. Repeat process with remaining eggs and filling. Serves 2.

Per serving: 109 cal. (41% from fat); 13.2 g protein; 5 g fat (1.55 g sat.); 1.3 g carbo.; 209 mg sodium; 213 mg chol.; 0 g fiber. Exchanges: 2 lean meat.

Asparagus-Parmesan Omelet Filling

Serve for breakfast, lunch or dinner.

½ cup steamed fresh asparagus pieces
2 tablespoons grated Parmesan cheese
1/16 teaspoon Morton Lite Salt® Mixture

Spoon ½ of the asparagus over each omelet, then sprinkle with Parmesan cheese and Morton Lite Salt® Mixture. Fold omelets over. Serves 2.

Per serving: 31 cal. (47% from fat); 2.9 g protein; 1.62 g fat (1 g sat.); 1.6 g carbo.; 130 mg sodium; 4 mg chol.; 0.31 g fiber. Exchanges: 1 vegetable.

Mushroom-Cheese Omelet Filling

A "lite" gourmet treat.

1 cup sliced mushrooms
1/16 teaspoon Morton Lite Salt® Mixture
2 tablespoons grated Parmesan cheese

In a heavy skillet sprayed with nonstick spray, stir-fry mushrooms over high heat until browned. Sprinkle with Morton Lite Salt® Mixture. Spoon ½ of the filling over each omelet, then sprinkle with Parmesan cheese. Fold omelets over. Serves 2.

Per serving: 32 cal. (46% from fat); 2.8 g protein; 1.65 g fat (0.98 g sat.); 1.8 g carbo.; 130 mg sodium; 4 mg chol.; 0.9 g fiber. Exchanges: 1 vegetable.

Spanish Omelet Filling

Slightly spicy and easy to prepare.

½ cup canned stewed tomatoes with onions and peppers (with juice)
1-2 drops hot pepper sauce
½ tablespoon cornstarch, dissolved in 2 tablespoons water
¼ cup grated fat-free cheddar cheese

In a small saucepan, simmer stewed tomatoes with hot pepper sauce and dissolved cornstarch, stirring constantly, until thickened. Spoon ½ over each omelet. Top with grated cheese. Fold omelets over. Serves 2.

Per serving: 38 cal. (5% from fat); 5 g protein; 0.2 g fat (0 g sat.); 4.5 g carbo.; 210 mg sodium; 2.5 mg chol.; 0.5 g fiber. Exchanges: 1 vegetable.

Spinach-Pimiento Omelet Filling

A visually appealing gastronomical treat.

3 tablespoons chopped green onion
½ package (10 oz.) frozen chopped spinach, thawed and squeezed dry
¼ teaspoon dried thyme leaves
3 tablespoons canned, diced pimiento
¼ cup grated fat-free mozzarella cheese

In a heavy skillet sprayed with nonstick spray, stir-fry green onion over medium heat until soft. Add spinach and thyme, then heat through. Add pimiento and mix. Spoon ½ of the filling over each omelet. Sprinkle with grated cheese. Fold omelets over. Serves 2.

Per serving: 48 cal. (7% from fat); 7.3 g protein; 0.39 g fat (0.06 g sat.); 5.6 g carbo.; 96 mg sodium; 2.5 mg chol.; 4.6 g fiber. Exchanges: ½ lean meat, 1 vegetable.

Avocado-Bacon-Cheese Omelet Filling

A rich-tasting blend of delectable flavors.

⅛ large, ripe avocado, peeled and cut into ½" cubes
¼ cup grated fat-free jack or mozzarella cheese
1 tablespoon lean cooked bacon bits
½ teaspoon Original Blend Mrs. Dash® seasoning

Mix all ingredients together. Spoon ½ of the filing over each omelet, then fold omelets over. Serves 2.

Per serving: 42 cal. (43% from fat); 5 g protein; 2 g fat (0.34 g sat.); 1.27 g carbo.; 124 mg sodium; 3.5 mg chol.; 0.23 g fiber. Exchanges: 1 lean meat.

Glazed Canadian Bacon

An elegant brunch dish.

1½ pounds Canadian bacon, with rind removed (if attached)
1 tablespoon Dijon mustard
Sugar substitute equal to 2 tablespoons brown sugar (i.e., 2 tablespoons Brown SugarTwin®)
1 tablespoon whole cloves

Mix mustard and sugar substitute, then spread over bacon. Stick cloves evenly over the top of the bacon. Place in a shallow baking pan sprayed with nonstick spray. Bake in a preheated 350° oven for 20 to 25 minutes, basting twice with mustard glaze from pan. Slice into 16 slices. Serves 8 (2 slices per serving).

Per serving: 120 cal. (32% from fat); 18 g protein; 4.2 g fat (1.36 g sat.); 0.61 g carbo.; 987 mg sodium; 25 mg chol.; 0.01 g fiber. Exchanges: 2½ lean meat. Add ½ fat exchange to meal plan.

Turkey Sausage

Very "lite" and flavorful!

1 pound ground turkey breast
½ small onion, finely minced
1 egg white, beaten
1 teaspoon dried thyme leaves
½ teaspoon dried sage
¼ teaspoon poultry seasoning
⅛ teaspoon pepper
½ teaspoon Morton Lite Salt® Mixture, optional

Mix all ingredients together. Using wet hands, shape the mixture into 8 patties or links. In a large, heavy skillet over medium-high heat, brown the turkey on all sides until thoroughly cooked, about 8 minutes. Serves 4.

Per serving: 145 cal. (5% from fat); 29 g protein; 0.78 g fat (0.24 g sat.); 3.4 g carbo.; 70 mg sodium; 70 mg chol.; 0.2 g fiber. Exchanges: 4 lean meat. Add 2 fat exchanges to meal plan.

"Healthy" Bacon

A delicious, low-fat alternative.

8 ounces lean ham, sliced ⅛" thick

Place ham slices in a stack, then cut into long strips the same width as bacon. In a large, heavy skillet sprayed with nonstick spray, brown strips (in a single layer in the skillet) on both sides. Cook strips in several batches so that they are not crowded in the skillet. Respray skillet with nonstick spray for each batch. Serves 4.

Per serving: 77 cal. (32% from fat); 12 g protein; 2.75 g fat (0.91 g sat.); 0 g carbo.; 642 mg sodium; 16.6 mg chol.; 0 g fiber. Exchanges: 2 lean meat. Add ½ fat exchange to meal plan.

Hashed Brown Potatoes

4 medium potatoes, peeled and grated
¼ cup grated onion
1 tablespoon Butter Buds®
½ teaspoon Original Blend
  Mrs. Dash® seasoning
½ teaspoon Morton Lite Salt® Mixture

Rinse grated potatoes in colander to remove excess starch. Drain well on paper towels. Mix potatoes with remaining ingredients. Spray a large, heavy ovenproof skillet with nonstick spray. Pour in potato mixture, distributing evenly in skillet. Bake in a preheated 475° oven for 10 minutes. Remove from oven. Turn potatoes over and bake 5 minutes longer. Serves 4.

Per serving: 120 cal. (1% from fat); 2.46 g protein; 0.12 g fat (0.03 g sat.); 28 g carbo.; 251 mg sodium; 0 mg chol.; 2.36 g fiber. Exchanges: 2 bread.

Country-Style Potatoes

A hearty breakfast favorite.

4 medium red potatoes, cut into
  ½" cubes
1 cup each: chopped green bell pepper
  and onion
½ teaspoon each: Morton Lite Salt®
  Mixture and Original Blend
  Mrs. Dash® seasoning

Place cubed potatoes and chopped vegetables in a large, heavy skillet sprayed with nonstick spray. Spray vegetables with nonstick spray. Roast in a preheated 475° oven for 10 minutes. Remove from oven, stir to mix and respray vegetables with nonstick spray. Return to 475° oven and roast 10 minutes longer. Again, remove from oven, stir to mix and respray with nonstick spray. Roast at 475° 10 minutes longer. Remove from oven and sprinkle with Morton Lite Salt® Mixture and Mrs. Dash®. Stir to mix. Serves 4.

Per serving: 130 cal. (2% from fat); 3.9 g protein; 0.29 g fat (0.06 g sat.); 29.3 g carbo.; 159 mg sodium; 0 mg chol.; 3.85 g fiber. Exchanges: 2 bread.

Granola with Raisins

Serve with low-fat milk or sprinkle over fat-free yogurt.

2 cups uncooked old-fashioned oats
2 tablespoons sesame seeds
¼ cup each: raisins and shredded
  dried coconut
¼ teaspoon Morton Lite Salt® Mixture
  Sugar substitute equal to ¼ cup brown
  sugar (i.e., ¼ cup Brown SugarTwin®)

Mix oats with sesame seeds. Place on a large baking sheet and toast in a preheated 300° oven, stirring every 5 minutes, for 15 minutes. Add coconut and continue to toast in a 300° oven for 5 minutes longer, or until coconut is golden. Cool and add raisins, Morton Lite Salt® Mixture and sugar substitute. Serves 6 (⅓ cup per serving).

Per serving: 157 cal. (28% from fat); 5 g protein; 4.9 g fat (1.42 g sat.); 27 g carbo.; 60 mg sodium; 0 mg chol.; 0.45 g fiber. Exchanges: 2 bread, 1 fat.

Maple Syrup

Serve with your favorite pancakes, waffles or French toast.

1 cup unsweetened apple juice
1 teaspoon maple flavoring
1 teaspoon Butter Buds®
1 tablespoon cornstarch
Sugar substitute equal to ⅓ cup sugar
(i.e., 8 packets Equal®)

Add apple juice, maple flavoring, Butter Buds® and cornstarch to a small saucepan. Stir well to dissolve cornstarch. Cook over medium heat, stirring constantly, until thickened. Stir in sugar substitute. Syrup may be refrigerated for up to 1 week. Serves 6 (3 tablespoons per serving).

Per serving: 25 cal. (2% from fat); 0.03 g protein; 0.06 g fat (0.01 g sat.); 6.2 g carbo.; 1 mg sodium; 0 mg chol.; 0.08 g fiber. Exchanges: ⅓ fruit.

Dutch Baby Pancake

Top with Maple Syrup (see recipe above).

3½ cups peeled, cored and thinly sliced Golden Delicious apples
2 teaspoons ground cinnamon
Sugar substitute equal to ¼ cup brown sugar (i.e., ¼ cup Brown SugarTwin®)
3 eggs
2 egg whites
1 cup each: unbleached flour and nonfat milk

Heat a large, heavy skillet with ovenproof handle over medium-high heat. Then spray with nonstick spray. Add apple slices, cover and cook, stirring occasionally, until apples are translucent, about 5 minutes. Sprinkle with cinnamon and place skillet, uncovered, in a preheated 425° oven for 5 minutes. Meanwhile, mix sugar substitute, eggs, egg whites, flour and milk in a blender. Pour batter evenly over apples in skillet. Bake, uncovered, until pancake is puffy and golden, about 15 minutes. Cut into 6 wedges. Serves 6.

Per serving: 162 cal. (17% from fat); 8.1 g protein; 3 g fat (0.9 g sat.); 26.3 g carbo.; 71 mg sodium; 107 mg chol.; 1.58 g fiber. Exchanges: 1 lean meat, 2 fruit.

French Toast

A "slimmed-down" version of a breakfast favorite.

2 eggs
2 egg whites
¼ cup nonfat milk
1 teaspoon each: vanilla extract and ground cinnamon
8 thick-cut slices firm white bread

Mix eggs, egg whites, milk, vanilla and cinnamon. Dip bread slices into egg mixture. Heat a griddle or large skillet over medium-high heat, then spray with nonstick spray. Brown bread slices about 3 minutes on one side. Respray skillet with nonstick spray, then brown slices 3 minutes on other side. Serves 4.

Per serving: 214 cal. (21% from fat); 10.4 g protein; 5.1 g fat (1.58 g sat.); 31 g carbo.; 389 mg sodium; 107 mg chol.; 1.5 g fiber. Exchanges: 1 medium-fat meat, 2 bread.

Multigrain Waffles

A nutritious blend of healthful ingredients.

⅓ cup each: whole wheat flour, cornmeal and uncooked oats, quick or old-fashioned
1 teaspoon each: baking powder and Butter Buds®
½ teaspoon baking soda
¼ teaspoon Morton Lite Salt® Mixture
Sugar substitute equal to 2 tablespoons sugar (i.e., 3 packets Equal®)
1 egg
1 cup low-fat (1% fat) buttermilk

In a bowl, combine flour, cornmeal, oats, baking powder, Butter Buds®, baking soda, Morton Lite Salt® Mixture and sugar substitute. In another bowl, mix egg with buttermilk. Pour liquid into dry ingredients. Stir enough to moisten evenly. Heat an electric waffle iron on medium-high heat, then spray heavily with nonstick spray. Evenly spoon in ¼ of batter. Close lid and cook for about 4 minutes. Lift out waffle, respray iron heavily with nonstick spray and repeat process with remaining batter. Serves 4.

Per serving: 113 cal. (20% from fat); 6.1 g protein; 2.5 g fat (0.75 g sat.); 17.2 g carbo.; 384 mg sodium; 56 mg chol.; 2.15 g fiber. Exchanges: ½ low-fat milk, ⅔ bread.

Blueberry Pancakes

Blueberries add color and flavor to this dish.

½ cup each: unbleached and whole wheat flour
½ teaspoon Morton Lite Salt® Mixture
½ tablespoon baking powder
Sugar substitute equal to 1 tablespoon sugar (i.e., 1½ packets Equal®)
1 cup nonfat milk
1 egg
½ tablespoon canola oil
1 cup blueberries, fresh or frozen (thawed)

In a mixing bowl, combine flours, Morton Lite Salt® Mixture, baking powder and sugar substitute. Mix milk, egg and oil. Stir milk mixture into flour mixture until barely mixed. For each pancake, pour ¼ cup pancake batter onto a hot griddle sprayed with nonstick spray. Next, sprinkle blueberries on top of each pancake. When cakes stop bubbling and are browned on the bottom, turn over with a spatula and cook on other side until browned. Respray griddle with nonstick spray as needed. Serves 4 (2 pancakes per serving).

Per serving: 180 cal. (18% fat); 7.4 g protein; 3.65 g fat (0.66 g sat.); 30 g carbo.; 194 mg sodium; 54 mg chol.; 3.5 g fiber. Exchanges: 2 bread, ½ fat.

Cottage Cheese Pancakes

These are delicious topped with Cinnamon Applesauce (see p. 90).

2 eggs, beaten
1 cup low-fat (1% fat) cottage cheese
1 cup low-fat (2% fat) yogurt
1 tablespoon vanilla extract
1 teaspoon finely grated lemon or
   orange rind
½ cup each: unbleached and whole
   wheat flour
½ teaspoon Morton Lite Salt® Mixture
   Sugar substitute equal to 2 tablespoons
   sugar (i.e., 3 packets Equal®)

Mix eggs, cottage cheese, yogurt, vanilla and grated rind. In a separate bowl, mix flours, Morton Lite Salt® Mixture and sugar substitute. Combine 2 mixtures. Spoon circles of batter onto a hot griddle or skillet sprayed with nonstick spray. Bake on both sides until golden brown. These may be made ahead of time and reheated before serving. Makes 12 pancakes. Serves 6.

Per serving: 144 cal. (18% from fat); 11 g protein; 2.9 g fat (1.17 g sat.); 18.6 g carbo.; 267 mg sodium; 75 mg chol.; 1.35 g fiber. Exchanges: 1½ lean meat, 1 bread.

Hearty Bran Pancakes

Serve with sugar-free Spiced Apple Butter (see p. 119).

⅓ cup whole wheat flour
⅓ cup miller's bran
2 teaspoons baking powder
¼ teaspoon Morton Lite Salt® Mixture
1 teaspoon canola oil
1 egg
1 cup nonfat milk

Mix flour, bran, baking powder and Morton Lite Salt® Mixture. In a separate bowl, mix oil, egg and milk, then combine with flour mixture. Spoon batter onto a large, hot skillet or griddle sprayed with nonstick spray. Cook over medium-high heat for about one minute, until bubbles that form in pancakes nearly open. Turn over and cook ½ minute longer. Makes 6 pancakes. Serves 3.

Per serving: 144 cal. (23% from fat); 7.7 g protein; 3.6 g fat (0.76 g sat.); 20 g carbo.; 519 mg sodium; 72 mg chol.; 3.1 g fiber. Exchanges: 1½ bread, ½ fat.

Carrot-Zucchini Muffins

The vegetables in these muffins add extra flavor, fiber and vitamins.

¾ cup each: unbleached and whole wheat flour
½ cup uncooked oats, quick or old-fashioned
Sugar substitute equal to ¼ cup brown sugar (i.e., ¼ cup Brown SugarTwin®)
1 teaspoon baking powder
½ teaspoon baking soda
⅓ cup raisins
¼ cup chopped walnuts, optional
1 tablespoon finely grated orange or lemon rind, optional
1 cup each: medium-grated raw carrot and raw zucchini
1½ cups low-fat (1% fat) buttermilk
1 egg
2 tablespoons honey (or an equivalent amount of sugar substitute, i.e., 2 tablespoons Brown SugarTwin®)
1 tablespoon vanilla extract

In a large mixing bowl, combine flours, oats, sugar substitute, baking powder and baking soda. Stir in raisins, nuts (if used), grated rind (if used), carrot and zucchini. In a blender, mix buttermilk, egg, honey and vanilla. Pour over premixed dry ingredients. Stir only until mixed. Add more buttermilk if batter is too dry. Spray muffin tins with nonstick spray. Fill tins ⅔ full. Bake in a preheated 400° oven for 15 to 20 minutes, or until done. Makes 12 muffins.

Per muffin: 111 cal. (10% from fat); 4.2 g protein; 1.18 g fat (0.34 g sat.); 22 g carbo.; 42 mg sodium; 19 mg chol.; 1.72 g fiber. Exchanges: 1½ bread.

Oat Bran Muffins

Hearty, healthful and full of fiber.

2 cups oat bran
1 cup each: unbleached and whole wheat flour
Sugar substitute equal to ½ cup brown sugar (i.e., ½ cup Brown SugarTwin®)
1 teaspoon each: baking soda, baking powder and ground cinnamon
½ teapoon each: ground allspice and Morton Lite Salt® Mixture
2 cups low-fat (1% fat) buttermilk
1 cup nonfat milk
1 egg
2 tablespoons canola oil
¼ cup raisins

In a large mixing bowl, combine bran, flours, sugar substitute, baking soda, baking powder, cinnamon, allspice and Morton Lite Salt® Mixture. In a blender, mix buttermilk, nonfat milk, egg and oil. Pour over premixed dry ingredients. Add raisins. Stir only until mixed. Add more buttermilk if batter is too dry. Spray muffin tins with nonstick spray. Fill tins ⅔ full. Bake in a preheated 400° oven for 15 to 20 minutes, or until done. Makes 18 muffins.

Per muffin: 119 cal. (22% from fat); 5.1 g protein; 2.94 g fat (0.39 g sat.); 18.6 g carbo.; 141 mg sodium; 13 mg chol.; 2.38 g fiber. Exchanges: 1 bread, ¼ low-fat milk.

Banana-Nut Muffins

These muffins freeze very well!

3 cups unbleached flour
1 cup whole wheat flour
1 teaspoon baking soda
4 teaspoons baking powder
½ teaspoon each: ground cinnamon and nutmeg
1 package (3 tablespoons) Butter Buds® Sugar substitute equal to ¼ cup brown sugar (i.e., ¼ cup Brown SugarTwin®)
4 ripe bananas
3 eggs
2 tablespoons canola oil
¼ cup honey (or an equivalent amount of sugar substitute, i.e., ¼ cup SugarTwin®)
2 cups nonfat milk
2 tablespoons chopped walnuts

In a large mixing bowl, combine flours, baking soda and baking powder, cinnamon, nutmeg, Butter Buds® and sugar substitute. In a blender, mix bananas, eggs, oil, honey and milk. Pour over premixed dry ingredients. Stir only until mixed. Add more milk if batter is too dry. Spray muffin tins with nonstick spray. Fill tins ⅔ full. Top with chopped nuts. Bake in a preheated 400° oven for 15 to 20 minutes, or until done. Makes 24 muffins.

Per muffin: 130 cal. (17% from fat); 4 g protein; 2.5 g fat (0.39 g sat.); 23.6 g carbo.; 40 mg sodium; 27 mg chol.; 1.47 g fiber. Exchanges: 1½ bread, ½ fat.

Cranberry-Prune Muffins

Moist and full of fruit.

¾ cup each: unbleached and whole wheat flour
1 teaspoon baking powder
½ teaspoon each: ground allspice, cinnamon and cloves
1 package (3 tablespoons) Butter Buds® Sugar substitute equal to 1 cup sugar (i.e., 1 cup SugarTwin®)
1 cup chopped moist-pack prunes
1 cup fresh or frozen cranberries, uncooked
2 eggs, beaten
1 cup water

In a large mixing bowl, combine flours, baking powder, allspice, cinnamon, cloves, Butter Buds® and sugar substitute. Stir in prune pieces and cranberries. Add eggs mixed with water. Stir only until mixed. Spray muffin tins with nonstick spray. Fill tins ⅔ full. Bake in a preheated 400° oven for 15 minutes, or until done. Makes 12 muffins.

Per muffin: 120 cal. (8% from fat); 3.3 g protein; 1.04 g fat (0.29 g sat.); 26 g carbo.; 55 mg sodium; 35.5 mg chol.; 3.2 g fiber. Exchanges: 1 bread, 1 fruit.

Sandwiches & Breads

Italian Supper Sandwiches

Satisfy hearty appetites with this dish.

1 pound lean ground beef
⅓ cup each: finely chopped onion and green pepper
½ cup tomato-based chili sauce
½ teaspoon Morton Lite Salt® Mixture
¼ teaspoon each: dried oregano and thyme leaves
1 long loaf (1 lb.) French bread, cut in half lengthwise
4 ounces fat-free mozzarella cheese, thinly sliced

Mix ground beef with onion, green pepper, chili sauce, Morton Lite Salt® Mixture, oregano and thyme. Spread the meat mixture on both halves of the French bread. Place on a large baking sheet and bake, uncovered, in a preheated 400° oven for 30 minutes. Arrange mozzarella slices on meat mixture, then return to oven for 2 minutes, or until cheese is barely melted. Cut into 8 slices. Serves 8.

Per serving: 271 cal. (29% from fat); 16.2 g protein; 8.8 g fat (3.1 g sat.); 30.6 g carbo.; 690 mg sodium; 30 mg chol.; 1.3 g fiber. Exchanges: 1½ medium-fat meat, 2 bread.

Easy Shrimp Sandwiches

Perfect for a quick, gourmet meal.

2 ounces medium cooked shrimp, cut into ½" pieces
½ cup grated fat-free mozzarella or cheddar cheese
2 tablespoons fat-free mayonnaise
1 tablespoon minced green onion
2 English muffins, cut in half and toasted

Mix shrimp, cheese, mayonnaise and green onion. Spread an equal amount of shrimp mixture on each toasted muffin half. Broil or microwave until cheese begins to melt. Serves 4.

Per serving: 120 cal. (6% from fat); 9.9 g protein; 0.75 g fat (0.2 g sat.); 14.2 g carbo.; 360 mg sodium; 24 mg chol.; 0.15 g fiber. Exchanges: 1 lean meat, 1 bread. Add 1 fat exchange to meal plan.

Reuben Sandwiches

A "lite" version of a classic favorite.

½ cup sauerkraut, drained
¼ cup shredded carrot
4 slices rye bread
4 slices (1 oz. each) lean, cooked corned beef
4 slices (¾ oz. each) fat-free Swiss cheese

Mix sauerkraut and carrot. On bread slices, arrange corned beef, then sauerkraut mixture, and top with Swiss cheese. Broil or microwave until cheese barely melts. Serves 4.

Per serving: 140 cal. (24% from fat); 11.7 g protein; 3.76 g fat (1.13 g sat.); 15.8 g carbo.; 685 mg sodium; 17.8 mg chol.; 1.5 g fiber. Exchanges: 1 lean meat, 1 bread.

Tuna Melt Sandwiches

Melted cheese adds a creamy-rich flavor.

1 can (6 oz.) water-packed tuna, drained
¼ cup each: minced celery and mild onion
¼ cup sweet pickle relish, optional
2 tablespoons fat-free mayonnaise
2 6" submarine rolls, cut in half lengthwise
1 medium tomato, cored and thinly sliced, optional
4 slices (1 oz. each) fat-free Swiss or American cheese

Mix tuna, celery, onion, pickle relish (if used) and mayonnaise. Spread an equal amount on the cut side of each roll. Top with tomato slices (if used), then 1 cheese slice per sandwich. Broil or microwave sandwiches until cheese begins to melt. Serves 4.

Per serving: 220 cal. (13% from fat); 23.3 g protein; 3.1 g fat (0.73 g sat.); 20 g carbo.; 457 mg sodium; 29 mg chol.; 0.62 g fiber. Exchanges: 2½ lean meat, 1 bread, 1 vegetable. Add 1 fat exchange to meal plan.

Vegetarian Delight

A fresh-tasting, healthful treat.

1 medium avocado, peeled and mashed
1 tablespoon lemon juice
¼ teaspoon Morton Lite Salt® Mixture
⅛ teaspoon pepper
1 clove garlic, minced
1 green onion, minced
¼ cup celery, minced
4 slices whole wheat bread
2 large mushrooms, sliced
½ cup alfalfa sprouts
1 medium tomato, sliced
4 thin slices (1 oz. each) fat-free Swiss cheese

Mix avocado, lemon juice, Morton Lite Salt® Mixture, pepper, garlic, green onion and celery. Spread ¼ of mixture on each slice of bread. Arrange mushrooms over avocado mixture. Top with alfalfa sprouts, tomato slices, then cheese. Broil sandwiches until cheese barely melts—about 2 minutes. Serves 4.

Per serving: 193 cal. (40% from fat); 12.6 g protein; 8.6 g fat (1.54 g sat.); 18.3 g carbo.; 425 mg sodium; 5 mg chol.; 3.7 g fiber. Exchanges: 1 high-fat meat, 1 bread, 1 vegetable.

Turkey-Pesto Sandwiches

Serve with soup or a salad.

1 long loaf (1 lb.) French bread, cut in half lengthwise
1 recipe Lite Pesto Sauce (see p. 87)
10 ounces cooked turkey or chicken breast, cut into ½" cubes
1½ cups grated fat-free mozzarella cheese (6 oz.)

Spread both halves of the French bread with pesto sauce. Scatter the cooked meat over the sauce, then top with grated cheese. Broil until cheese melts. Serves 8.

Per serving: 273 cal. (25% from fat); 19.2 g protein; 7.6 g fat (2 g sat.); 28.7 g carbo.; 689 mg sodium; 28 mg chol.; 2.03 g fiber. Exchanges: 2 lean meat, 2 bread.

Chicken Salad Sandwiches

A nutritious blend—so good for you!

1½ cups diced cooked chicken
1 hard-boiled egg, chopped
¼ cup fat-free mayonnaise
2 tablespoons each: minced celery and stuffed green olives
1 tablespoon each: sweet pickle relish and minced green onion
⅛ teaspoon Morton Lite Salt® Mixture
12 slices light wheat or white bread

In a medium bowl, combine all ingredients except bread. Spread 6 slices of bread with chicken mixture and top with remaining slices. Serves 6.

Per serving: 192 cal. (24% from fat); 17.2 g protein; 5.2 g fat (1.01 g sat.); 15.2 g carbo.; 451 mg sodium; 67 mg chol.; 4.1 g fiber. Exchanges: 2 lean meat, 1 bread.

Monte Cristo Sandwiches

Rich-tasting, yet low in fat.

1 tablespoon each: fat-free mayonnaise and catsup
2 ounces roasted chicken breast, thinly sliced
2 thin slices (¾ oz. each) fat-free Swiss cheese
4 slices rye bread
1 egg, beaten
¼ cup nonfat milk

Mix mayonnaise and catsup, then spread on 2 slices of bread. Top with chicken, then cheese. Cover with the remaining bread slices. Mix egg and milk. Dip sandwiches into egg mixture. Then brown on both sides, over medium-high heat, in a large, heavy skillet sprayed with nonstick spray. Serves 2.

Per serving: 266 cal. (17% from fat); 19.4 g protein; 5 g fat (1.31 g sat.); 30.5 g carbo.; 694 mg sodium; 128 mg chol.; 2.25 g fiber. Exchanges: 2 lean meat, 2 bread.

Easy Chicken Fajitas

Full of flavor and easy to prepare.

½ pound boneless, skinless chicken breasts, cut into ½" cubes
3 tablespoons fresh lemon or lime juice
1 clove garlic, minced
½ teaspoon dried oregano leaves
¼ teaspoon ground cumin
½ cup each: diced onion and green bell pepper
4 flour or corn tortillas
⅔ cup grated fat-free cheddar cheese
½ cup salsa
¼ cup chopped fresh cilantro

Marinate chicken cubes in a mixture of lemon or lime juice, garlic, oregano and cumin for 1 hour. In a large, heavy skillet sprayed with nonstick spray, stir-fry chicken over medium-high heat until cooked through. Remove from skillet and keep warm. Respray skillet with nonstick spray and stir-fry onion and pepper until tender. Return chicken to skillet. Stir to mix. Warm tortillas in a microwave oven. Spoon an equal amount of chicken-vegetable mixture down the center of each tortilla. Top with grated cheese, salsa and cilantro. Fold over to serve. Serves 4.

Per serving: 252 cal. (14% from fat); 17.6 g protein; 3.8 g fat (0.57 g sat.); 32 g carbo.; 684 mg sodium; 35.5 mg chol.; 5.1 g fiber. Exchanges: 1½ lean meat, 2 bread.

Grilled Chicken Burgers

A "slimmed-down" version of an American favorite.

1 tablespoon each: cornstarch, low-sodium soy sauce and chopped fresh parsley
Sugar substitute equal to 1 teaspoon sugar (i.e., ½ packet Equal®)
1 pound ground chicken breast
1 clove minced garlic
1 green onion, minced
1 egg, beaten
½ teaspoon finely grated fresh ginger or dried ground ginger
6 hamburger buns
1 medium tomato, sliced
6 small lettuce leaves

In a large bowl, mix cornstarch with soy sauce, parsley and sugar substitute. Add chicken, garlic, green onion, egg and ginger. Mix well, then shape into 6 flat patties. Barbecue 4" from hot coals on a fine-mesh, nonstick grate for 3 minutes on each side, or until done. Or grill over high heat in a large, heavy skillet sprayed with nonstick spray for 3 minutes per side, or until done. Serve each patty on a hamburger bun with a tomato slice and lettuce leaf. Serves 6.

Per serving: 221 cal. (15% from fat); 15.5 g protein; 3.8 g fat (1 g sat.); 22.5 g carbo.; 314 mg sodium; 79 mg chol.; 0.46 g fiber. Exchanges: 1½ lean meat, 1½ bread.

Grilled Cheese Sandwich

Serve with a cup or bowl of savory, low-fat soup.

2 slices light bread
1 slice (1 oz.) fat-free American cheese

Place cheese inside slices of bread. Spray outside of bread with butter-flavored nonstick spray. Broil on both sides until bread is toasted and cheese is melted. Serves 1.

Per serving: 120 cal. (0% from fat); 13 g protein; 0 g fat (0 g sat.); 21 g carbo.; 400 mg sodium; 5 mg chol.; 4 g fiber. Exchanges: 1 lean meat, 1½ bread. Add ½ fat exchange to meal plan.

Garlic-Dill French Bread

A delicious addition to any meal!

6 slices (1 oz. each) French bread
2 tablespoons fat-free margarine
½ teaspoon each: garlic powder and dried dillweed
2 tablespoons grated Parmesan cheese

Spread each slice of bread with 1 teaspoon margarine. Sprinkle garlic powder and dill over each slice. Sprinkle 1 teaspoon Parmesan cheese over each slice. Microwave or broil only until margarine and cheese are melted. Serves 6.

Per serving: 89 cal. (15% from fat); 2.7 g protein; 1.5 g fat (0.52 g sat.); 13 g carbo.; 209 mg sodium; 1.33 mg chol.; 0.6 g fiber. Exchanges: 1 bread.

Corn Bread

You'll love this moist, slightly sweet bread.

1 cup yellow cornmeal
1 cup unbleached flour
1 tablespoon baking powder
½ teaspoon Morton Lite Salt® Mixture
   Sugar substitute equal to 3 tablespoons sugar (i.e., 3 tablespoons SugarTwin®)
1 egg
1 cup low-fat (1% fat) buttermilk
½ cup unsweetened applesauce

In a mixing bowl, combine dry ingredients. Mix egg, buttermilk and applesauce together. Add to dry ingredients, and stir to mix. Pour into a square 8" pan sprayed with nonstick spray. Bake in a preheated 400° oven for 20 to 25 minutes, or until a toothpick inserted in center comes out clean. Serves 8.

Per serving: 96 cal. (10% from fat); 3.64 g protein; 1.1 g fat (0.39 g sat.); 17.5 g carbo.; 73 mg sodium; 28 mg chol.; 2.1 g fiber. Exchanges: 1 bread.

Beverages

Strawberry Smoothie

Serve for breakfast or as a snack anytime.

1 cup artificially sweetened, vanilla-flavored nonfat yogurt
½ cup nonfat milk
3 cups strawberries
  Sugar substitute equal to ¼ cup sugar (i.e., 6 packets Equal®)
1 cup ice cubes

In a blender, combine all ingredients until smooth. Serves 3.

Per serving: 104 cal. (6% from fat); 6 g protein; 0.67 g fat (0.08 g sat.); 20 g carbo.; 76 mg sodium; 0.67 mg chol.; 3 g fiber. Exchanges: ½ nonfat milk, 1 fruit.

Banana-Orange Smoothie

A delicious blend of orange and banana flavors.

1 cup artificially sweetened, vanilla-flavored nonfat yogurt
½ cup nonfat milk
1 cup unsweetened orange juice
1 medium banana
  Sugar substitute equal to ¼ cup sugar (i.e., 6 packets Equal®)
1 cup ice cubes

In a blender, combine all ingredients until smooth. Serves 3.

Per serving: 131 cal. (2% from fat); 6 g protein; 0.31 g fat (0.12 g sat.); 27 g carbo.; 75 mg sodium; 0.67 mg chol.; 1.33 g fiber. Exchanges: ½ nonfat milk, 1½ fruit.

Peach Smoothie

A luscious peach-flavored drink.

1 cup artificially sweetened, vanilla-flavored nonfat yogurt
½ cup nonfat milk
3 medium peaches, peeled and pitted
  Sugar substitute equal to ¼ cup sugar (i.e., 6 packets Equal®)
1 cup ice cubes

In a blender, combine all ingredients until smooth. Serves 3.

Per serving: 96 cal. (2% from fat); 5.7 g protein; 0.17 g fat (0.06 g sat.); 19 g carbo.; 205 mg sodium; 0.67 mg chol.; 2 g fiber. Exchanges: ½ nonfat milk, 1 fruit.

Pineapple-Banana Smoothie

Tropical flavor abounds.

1 cup artificially sweetened,
   vanilla-flavored nonfat yogurt
½ cup nonfat milk
¾ cup juice-pack pineapple
1 medium banana
   Sugar substitute equal to ¼ cup sugar
   (i.e., 6 packets Equal®)
1 cup ice cubes

In a blender, combine all ingredients until smooth. Serves 3.

Per serving: 132 cal. (2% from fat); 5.7 g protein; 0.32 g fat (0.11 g sat.); 28 g carbo.; 76 mg sodium; 0.67 mg chol.; 1.5 g fiber. Exchanges: 1 nonfat milk, 1 fruit.

Cinnamon-Apple Smoothie

Tastes like a milk shake.

1 cup artificially sweetened,
   vanilla-flavored nonfat yogurt
½ cup nonfat milk
1½ cups unsweetened applesauce
   Sugar substitute equal to ¼ cup sugar
   (i.e., 6 packets Equal®)
   Dash ground cinnamon
1 cup ice cubes

In a blender, combine all ingredients until smooth. Serves 3.

Per serving: 112 cal. (1% from fat); 5.3 g protein; 0.17 g fat (0.06 g sat.); 23 g carbo.; 76 mg sodium; 0.67 mg chol.; 0.7 g fiber. Exchanges: ½ nonfat milk, 1 fruit.

Peach Nectar Spritzer

A light, refreshing drink.

1½ cups (12 oz.) peach nectar
½ cup unsweetened orange juice
2 cups diet grapefruit-flavored soda
4 sprigs mint, optional

Mix liquid ingredients together and serve with ice and a mint garnish (if used). Serves 4.

Per serving: 65 cal. (1% from fat); 0.47 g protein; 0.05 g fat (0.01 g sat.); 16.3 g carbo.; 6.6 mg sodium; 0 mg chol.; 0.27 g fiber. Exchanges: 1 fruit.

Cranberry Spritzer

A healthful, low-calorie drink.

2 cups low-calorie cranberry
   juice cocktail
2 cups diet lemon-lime soda

Mix together and serve with ice. Serves 4.

Per serving: 25 cal. (0% from fat); 0 g protein; 0 g fat (0 g sat.); 6 g carbo.; 5 mg sodium; 0 mg chol.; 0 g fiber. Exchanges: ⅓ fruit.

Lemon Spritzer

Delicious on a hot day!

¾ cup fresh lemon juice
 4 cups plain soda
    Sugar substitute equal to ⅓ cup sugar
    (i.e., 8 packets Equal®), or
    more to taste

Mix together and serve with ice. Serves 4.

Per serving: 18 cal. (7% from fat); 0.18 g protein; 0.13 g fat (0.02 g sat.); 5 g carbo.; 9.4 mg sodium; 0 mg chol.; 0.03 g fiber. Exchanges: ⅓ fruit.

Citrus Spritzer

½ cup each: unsweetened grapefruit juice
   and orange juice
2 cups diet lemon-lime soda
   Sugar substitute equal to 2 tablespoons
   sugar (i.e., 3 packets Equal®), or more
   to taste

Mix together and serve with ice. Serves 3.

Per serving: 29 cal. (2% from fat); 0.36 g protein; 0.05 g fat (0.01 g sat.); 6.6 g carbo.; 0.5 mg sodium; 0 mg chol.; 0.08 g fiber. Exchanges: ⅓ fruit.

Triple-Fruit Spritzer

A great thirst quencher!

2 tablespoons lemon juice
1 cup each: unsweetened pineapple juice
   and orange juice
2 cups diet ginger ale
   Sugar substitute equal to 2 tablespoons
   sugar (i.e., 3 packets Equal®), or more to taste

Mix together and serve with ice. Serves 4.

Per serving: 68 cal. (1% from fat); 0.65 g protein; 0.1 g fat (0.01 g sat.); 16.5 g carbo.; 3.4 mg sodium; 0 mg chol.; 0.33 g fiber. Exchanges: 1 fruit.

Spicy Tomato-Juice Cocktail

Full of flavor, with a spicy tang.

3 cups tomato juice
1 tablespoon each: lemon juice and Worcestershire sauce
2 drops hot pepper sauce
3 small celery stalks

Mix liquid ingredients together. Serve well chilled, with a celery stalk in each glass. Serves 3.

Per serving: 47 cal. (2% from fat); 2.2 g protein; 0.11 g fat (0.02 g sat.); 10.7 g carbo.; 487 mg sodium; 0 mg chol.; 1.7 g fiber. Exchanges: 1 vegetable, ⅓ fruit.

Oriental Punch

A delicately seasoned beverage.

6 whole cloves
1 cinnamon stick
½ teaspoon dried ground ginger or finely grated fresh ginger
2 cups water
½ cup fresh mint leaves
1 cup unsweetened orange juice
⅓ cup fresh lemon juice
  Sugar substitute equal to ½ cup sugar (i.e., 12 packets Equal®)
2½ cups ice cubes
4 mint sprigs

Combine cloves, cinnamon stick, ginger and water in a saucepan; boil for 3 minutes. Add mint leaves; cover, and let stand until cool. Strain, and add orange juice, lemon juice and sugar substitute. Pour over ice cubes in 4 glasses and garnish with mint sprigs. Serves 4.

Per serving: 43 cal. (1% from fat); 0.49 g protein; 0.07 g fat (0.01 g sat.); 10.7 g carbo.; 3.6 mg sodium; 0 mg chol.; 0.26 g fiber. Exchanges: ⅔ fruit.

Spiced Iced Tea

Serve anytime.

4 cups boiling water
2 tea bags, decaf or regular
2 whole cloves
½ cinnamon stick
2 teaspoons grated lemon peel
  Sugar substitute to taste (i. e., Equal®)
  Ice cubes

Mix all ingredients, except ice, and allow to brew for 5 minutes. Remove tea bags. Cool, then strain into 4 glasses filled with ice. Serves 4.

Per serving: 1 cal. (9% from fat); 0.02 g protein; 0.01 g fat (0 g sat.); 0.39 g carbo.; 0.09 mg sodium; 0 mg chol.; 0 g fiber. Exchanges: Free.

Hot Cranberry Punch

Cinnamon, cloves and allspice add flavor to this punch.

2	cups low-calorie cranberry juice
2	cups unsweetened pineapple juice
2¼	cups water
1	tablespoon whole cloves
3	cinnamon sticks, broken in half
1½	teaspoons whole allspice
	(or ½ teaspoon ground allspice)
	Sugar substitute equal to ½ cup brown
	sugar (i.e., ½ cup Brown SugarTwin®)

In a covered saucepan, simmer cranberry juice, pineapple juice, water, cloves, cinnamon sticks, allspice and sugar substitute for 10 minutes. Strain into 6 cups. Serves 6.

Per serving: 70 cal. (1% from fat); 0.27 g protein; 0.07 g fat (0 g sat.); 17.5 g carbo.; 4 mg sodium; 0 mg chol.; 0.1 g fiber. Exchanges: 1 fruit.

Hot Spiced Fruit Punch

A healthful blend of juices for any special occasion.

2	cups unsweetened orange juice
2	cups apple cider
2	cups low-calorie cranberry juice
2	cinnamon sticks
½	teaspoon whole cloves
	Sugar substitute equal to ¼ cup
	brown sugar (i.e., ¼ cup Brown
	SugarTwin®)
6	thin orange slices

In a covered saucepan, simmer orange juice, apple cider, cranberry juice, cinnamon sticks, cloves and sugar substitute for 5 minutes. Strain into 6 cups and garnish with orange slices. Serves 6.

Per serving: 133 cal. (1% from fat); 0.72 g protein; 0.17 g fat (0.03 g sat.); 34 g carbo.; 6.3 mg sodium; 0 mg chol.; 0.76 g fiber. Exchanges: 2 fruit.

Hot Pineapple Cider

Mint, pineapple and cider—a delicious combination.

2	cups apple cider
1	cup unsweetened pineapple juice
½	cup fresh mint leaves
2	cups diet ginger ale

In a saucepan, combine apple cider, pineapple juice and mint leaves. Bring to a boil. Strain, and add unchilled ginger ale. Serve warm. Serves 5.

Per serving: 82 cal. (2% from fat); 0.62 g protein; 0.15 g fat (0.02 g sat.); 20.5 g carbo.; 7.6 mg sodium; 0 mg chol.; 0.38 g fiber. Exchanges: 1⅓ fruit.

Hot Mulled Cider

Delicious served on a cold day.

4 cups apple cider
4 thin slices each: lemon and orange with peel
8 whole cloves
½ teaspoon each: ground cinnamon and nutmeg
4 cinnamon sticks, optional

In a saucepan, combine cider, lemon and orange slices, cloves, ground cinnamon and nutmeg. Simmer for 5 minutes. Remove from heat and let stand for 5 minutes. Strain into mugs and serve hot; garnish with cinnamon sticks (if used). Serves 4.

Per serving: 123 cal. (3% from fat); 0.23 g protein; 0.38 g fat (0.06 g sat.); 32 g carbo.; 7.9 mg sodium; 0 mg chol.; 0.92 g fiber. Exchanges: 2 fruit.

Holiday Punch

A party drink that's great for entertaining.

6 cups apple cider
2 cups unsweetened orange juice
1 medium orange, sliced
1 tablespoon lemon juice
4 cinnamon sticks
2 teaspoons whole cloves
½ teaspoon ground allspice (or 1½ teaspoons whole allspice)
1 cup water

In a large saucepan, combine all ingredients. Cover and simmer for 1 hour. Strain, and serve hot. Serves 8.

Per serving: 128 cal. (2% from fat); 0.7 g protein; 0.27 g fat (0.04 g sat.); 33 g carbo.; 6.5 mg sodium; 0 mg chol.; 1.2 g fiber. Exchanges: 2 fruit.

Hot Spiced Tea

Tea with a flavorful blend of spices.

4 cups boiling water
2 tea bags, decaf or regular
½ teaspoon whole cloves
1 cinnamon stick
2 cups unsweetened orange juice
1 tablespoon lemon juice
Sugar substitute to taste (i. e., Equal®)

In a saucepan, mix boiling water with tea bags, cloves and cinnamon stick. Cover pan, and let brew for 5 minutes. Remove tea bags. Add remaining ingredients, and heat until warm. Strain into 6 cups. Serves 6.

Per serving: 53 cal. (1% from fat); 0.69 g protein; 0.06 g fat (0.01 g sat.); 13 g carbo.; 3.5 mg sodium; 0.57 mg chol.; 0.57 g fiber. Exchanges: 1 fruit.

Coffee Supreme

Rich-tasting and satisfying!

2 cups hot coffee, instant or brewed, decaf or regular
  Sugar substitute to taste, optional (i. e., Equal®)
¼ cup "lite" whipped topping
½ teaspoon unsweetened cocoa powder
¼ teaspoon finely grated orange peel

Pour hot coffee into 2 cups and add sugar substitute (if used). Top with whipped topping. Using a small strainer, sprinkle topping with cocoa powder, and then add grated orange peel. Serves 2.

Per serving: 27 cal. (67% from fat); 2 g protein; 2 g fat (0.05 g sat.); 2.63 g carbo.; 8.6 mg sodium; 0.17 mg chol.; 0 g fiber. Exchanges: ½ vegetable, ½ fat.

Mocha Dessert Coffee

A special treat your guests will enjoy.

2 teaspoons instant coffee, decaf or regular
1 package (0.53 oz.) fat- and sugar-free hot cocoa mix
1 cup low-fat (1% fat) milk, heated
1 cup boiling water
  Sugar substitute equal to 1 tablespoon sugar (i.e., 1½ packets Equal®), or more to taste

Dissolve coffee and cocoa mix in hot milk. Add boiling water and sugar substitute and pour into 2 cups. Serves 2.

Per serving: 80 cal. (15% from fat); 5.5 g protein; 1.3 g fat (0.8 g sat.); 11.3 g carbo.; 164 mg sodium; 5 mg chol.; 0.5 g fiber. Exchanges: 1 nonfat milk.

Mexican Coffee

Cinnamon and nutmeg add a delicious spiciness.

2 cups hot coffee, instant or brewed, decaf or regular
  Sugar substitute to taste (i. e., Equal®)
½ teaspoon ground cinnamon
¼ cup "lite" whipped topping
⅛ teaspooon each: ground cinnamon and nutmeg
2 cinnamon sticks, optional

Mix coffee, sugar substitute and ½ teaspoon ground cinnamon, then pour into two cups. Top each with a dollop of whipped topping. Sprinkle topping with cinnamon and nutmeg. Garnish each cup with a cinnamon stick (if used). Serves 2.

Per serving: 25 cal. (72% from fat); 2 g protein; 2 g fat (0 g sat.); 2.4 g carbo.; 5.4 mg sodium; 0 mg chol.; 0 g fiber. Exchanges: ½ fat.

Preserves & Condiments

Strawberry Jam

A fresh-tasting preserve.

2 quarts strawberries, washed and with stems removed

1 package (1¾ oz.) low-methoxyl pectin (gels without sugar)

Sugar substitute equal to 1½ cups sugar (i.e., 36 packets Equal®)

Mash strawberries. In a large, heavy pot, mix strawberries and pectin. Let stand 10 minutes, then cook, stirring constantly, until mixture comes to a boil. Boil 1 minute. Remove from heat. Mix in sugar substitute. Use within 1 week or freeze in 1-cup containers. Serves 16 (2 tablespoons per serving).

Per serving: 16 cal. (8% from fat); 0.25 g protein; 0.15 g fat (0 g sat.); 3.8 g carbo.; 1 mg sodium; 0 mg chol.; 0.75 g fiber. Exchanges: Free for 1 serving.

Quick Berry Jam

Delicious with your morning toast.

1½ cups fresh or frozen raspberries or crushed blackberries

1½ tablespoons cornstarch

⅓ cup water

Sugar substitute equal to ¼ cup sugar (i.e., 6 packets Equal®), or more to taste

Place berries in a heavy saucepan. Add cornstarch dissolved in water. Cook over medium heat, stirring constantly, until thickened. Remove from heat and let cool. Stir in sugar substitute. Refrigerate for up to 5 days or freeze for longer storage. Serves 12 (2 tablespoons per serving).

Per serving: 14 cal. (0% from fat); 0.15 g protein; 0 g fat (0 g sat.); 3.56 g carbo.; 0.04 mg sodium; 0 mg chol.; 2.27 g fiber. Exchanges: Free for 1 serving.

Super-Easy Marmalade

A special treat for breakfast!

1 orange, thinly sliced

1 lemon, thinly sliced

½ grapefruit, thinly sliced

1 cup water

2 tablespoons orange-flavored liqueur, optional

1 teaspoon ground cinnamon

Sugar substitute equal to ⅔ cup sugar (i.e., 16 packets Equal®), or more to taste

In a covered saucepan, simmer orange, lemon and grapefruit with water for 2 hours. Stir occasionally, and add more water, ¼ cup at a time, if marmalade becomes too dry. Add liqueur (if used) and simmer for ½ hour longer. Cool; add cinnamon and sugar substitute. Refrigerate for up to 1 week or freeze in 1-cup containers. Serves 20 (2 tablespoons per serving).

Per serving: 15 cal. (2% from fat); 0.13 g protein; 0.03 g fat (0.01 g sat.); 2.9 g carbo.; 0.25 mg sodium; 0 mg chol.; 0.2 g fiber. Exchanges: Free for 1 serving.

Apricot-Pineapple Jam

Full of flavor, but not full of calories.

½ cup dried apricots (3 oz.)
1 cup water
1 cup juice-pack crushed pineapple, with juice
1 tablespoon cornstarch, dissolved in 3 tablespoons water
Sugar substitute equal to ½ cup sugar (i.e., 12 packages Equal®)

In a small saucepan, simmer apricots with water, covered, for 45 minutes. Add crushed pineapple with juice and dissolved cornstarch and simmer, stirring constantly, until thickened. Remove from heat. Cool, and add sugar substitute. Chill before serving. Makes 16 servings (2 tablespoons per serving).

Per serving: 28 cal. (1% from fat); 0.19 g protein; 0.02 g fat (0 g sat.); 6.8 g carbo.; 27 mg sodium; 0 mg chol.; 0.38 g fiber. Exchanges: ½ fruit.

Spiced Apple Butter

Serve as a topping for French toast, pancakes or waffles.

5 cups unsweetened applesauce
1 teaspoon ground cinnamon
½ teaspoon ground cloves
1½ teaspoons each: finely grated orange and lemon rind
Sugar substitute equal to ⅔ cup brown sugar (i.e., ⅔ cup Brown SugarTwin®)

In a heavy, uncovered saucepan, simmer all ingredients over low heat, stirring frequently, until apple butter reaches the desired thickness—about 1 hour. Apple butter may be stored in the refrigerator for 1 week, or frozen or canned for longer storage. Makes 4 cups.

Per tablespoon: 10 cal. (1% from fat); 0.02 g protein; 0.01 g fat (0 g sat.); 1.72 g carbo.; 0.25 mg sodium; 0 mg chol.; 0.09 g fiber. Exchanges: Free for 2 tablespoons.

Orange-Prune Butter

So easy to fix, with lots of flavor and fiber!

½ cup (4 oz.) pitted prunes
⅓ cup orange juice
½ teaspoon ground cinnamon, optional

In a blender or food processor, mix prunes, juice and cinnamon (if used) until smooth. Serves 7 (2 tablespoons per serving).

Per serving: 48 cal. (0% from fat); 0.5 g protein; 0 g fat (0 g sat.); 12.4 g carbo.; 2.24 mg sodium; 0 mg chol.; 1.33 g fiber. Exchanges: 1 fruit.

Cranberry-Orange Relish

1 bag (12 oz.) cranberries
1 navel orange with peel, diced fine
(remove any seeds)
1½ cups water
¼ teaspoon ground cinnamon
Sugar substitute equal to 1½ cups sugar
(i.e., 36 packets Equal®), or more to taste

Simmer the cranberries and orange with water in a covered saucepan for 1 hour. Cool, and stir in cinnamon and sugar substitute. Refrigerate for up to 1 week or freeze in 1-cup containers. Serves 8.

Per serving: 25 cal. (4% from fat); 0.29 g protein; 0.1 g fat (0.01 g sat.); 6.4 g carbo.; 9 mg sodium; 0 mg chol.; 3.35 g fiber. Exchanges: ½ fruit.

Apricot Chutney

15 medium apricots, pitted (or substitute
3 oz. dried apricots)
½ cup chopped onion
½ dried, seeded red chili pepper
½ tablespoon finely grated fresh ginger
(or 1 teaspoon dried ground ginger)
1 clove garlic, minced
¼ cup cider vinegar
3 tablespoons raisins
Sugar substitute equal to ⅓ cup sugar
(i.e., ⅓ cup SugarTwin®)
½ teaspoon ground cinnamon
¼ teaspoon Morton Lite Salt® Mixture
Dash ground cumin

Mix all ingredients in a heavy saucepan and simmer, uncovered, until thickened. Serves 16.

Per serving: 21 cal. (6% from fat); 0.55 g protein; 0.14 g fat (0 g sat.); 5 g carbo.; 19 mg sodium; 0 mg chol.; 0.8 g fiber. Exchanges: ⅓ fruit.

Corn-Pepper Relish

2 cups corn (fresh, frozen or canned)
½ cup rice vinegar
½ cup each: chopped green and
red bell pepper
¼ cup each: chopped celery and onion
1 clove garlic, minced
¾ teaspoon Morton Lite Salt® Mixture
Sugar substitute equal to ¼ cup sugar
(i. e., 6 packets Equal®)

Combine all ingredients, except sugar substitute, in a saucepan. Bring to a boil and simmer for 3 minutes. Cool, add sugar substitute, and refrigerate. Makes 3 cups. Serves 12 (¼ cup per serving).

Per serving: 36 cal. (10% from fat); 1 g protein; 0.4 g fat (0.07 g sat.); 8.6 g carbo.; 79 mg sodium; 0 mg chol.; 1.77 g fiber. Exchanges: ½ bread.

Old-Fashioned Chili Sauce

6 pounds ripe tomatoes, peeled and
  cut into pieces
1 bell pepper, seeded and finely chopped
1 large onion, finely chopped
⅓ cup cider or rice vinegar
1 tablespoon Morton Lite Salt® Mixture
¼ teaspoon each: ground cinnamon,
  ground allspice and dry mustard
  Dash cayenne pepper
  Sugar substitute equal to ⅓ cup
  brown sugar (i.e., ⅓ cup Brown SugarTwin®)

Mix all ingredients together in a large, heavy saucepan. Simmer, uncovered, until thick— about 1 hour. Sauce may be refrigerated for 2 weeks, frozen or canned. Serves 30 (2 tablespoons per serving).

Per serving: 16 cal. (11% from fat); 0.73 g protein; 0.19 g fat (0.03 g sat.); 3.76 g carbo.; 121 mg sodium; 0 mg chol.; 0.95 g fiber. Exchanges: Free for 1 serving.

Ginger Pear Chips

2 large (firm, yet ripe) pears
⅓ cup water
1 tablespoon fresh lemon juice
1 teaspoon each: finely grated lemon rind
  and fresh ginger
  Sugar substitute equal to ¼ cup sugar
  (i.e., 6 packets Equal®)

Peel and slice pears. In a saucepan, simmer pear slices with water, lemon juice, grated lemon rind and ginger until barely tender. Remove from heat. Cool slightly, and gently stir in sugar substitute. Serve chilled. Serves 8 (¼ cup per serving).

Per serving: 26 cal. (6% from fat); 0.17 g protein; 0.16 g fat (0 g sat.); 6.6 g carbo.; 0.62 mg sodium; 0 mg chol.; 0.91 g fiber. Exchanges: ½ fruit.

Zucchini Pickles

Serve with your favorite sandwich.

3 medium zucchini, ends removed and
  cut into ⅛" slices
1 medium onion, cut into thin slices
¼ cup Morton Lite Salt® Mixture
2 teaspoons mustard seed
1 teaspoon each: ground turmeric and
  celery seed
  Sugar substitute equal to 1½ cups sugar
  (i.e., 1½ cups SugarTwin®)
2 cups cider vinegar

Place sliced zucchini and onion in a large pottery bowl with enough water to cover. Add Morton Lite Salt® Mixture, and stir to mix. Let stand 1 hour, then drain. Place zucchini and onion in a large, heavy pot with mustard seed, turmeric, celery seed, sugar substitute and vinegar. Bring to a boil and cook 3 minutes— until zucchini slices are barely tender. Store in refrigerator in glass jars for up to 1 month. Makes 24 servings.

Per serving: 6 cal. (5% from fat); 0.25 g protein; 0.03 g fat (0 g sat.); 1.9 g carbo; 145 mg sodium; 0 mg chol.; 0.57 g fiber. Exchanges: Free for 3 servings.

Dilled Green Beans

Serve as a snack, hors d'oeuvre or meal accompaniment.

2 pounds small, tender green beans,
  with stems removed
1 teaspoon red pepper flakes
4 cloves garlic
4 heads dill
¼ cup Morton Lite Salt® Mixture
2 cups each: water and rice vinegar

Pack green beans into 4 hot, sterilized pint-size glass canning jars. To each jar add ¼ teaspoon red pepper, 1 clove garlic, 1 head dill and 1 tablespoon Morton Lite Salt® Mixture. In a saucepan, bring water and vinegar to a boil. Pour over beans. Seal with canning lids, and process in a boiling water bath for 5 minutes. Serves 20.

Per serving: 16 cal. (5% from fat); 0.76 g protein; 0.09 g fat (0.02 g sat.); 3.9 g carbo.; 231 mg sodium; 0 mg chol.; 0.46 g fiber. Exchanges: Free for 1 serving.

Pickled Okra

Crunchy, tangy and delicious.

20 medium, tender okra, with stem
   end trimmed
1 clove garlic, minced
1 teaspoon each: Morton Lite Salt®
  Mixture, celery seed, dillseed and
  mustard seed
½ teaspoon red pepper flakes
1 cup each: cider vinegar and water

Tightly pack okra into 2 hot, sterilized pint-size glass canning jars. Add garlic, Morton Lite Salt® Mixture, celery seed, dillseed, mustard seed and red pepper flakes. Bring vinegar and water to a boil. Pour over okra in jars. Seal with canning lids, and process in a boiling water bath for 5 minutes. Serves 10.

Per serving: 9 cal. (10% from fat); 0.5 g protein; 0.1 g fat (0.02 g sat.); 2.1 g carbo.; 3.3 mg sodium; 0 mg chol.; 6 g fiber. Exchanges: Free for 2 servings.

Bell Pepper Relish

Good with sandwiches or meat dishes.

1 each: medium red and green bell
  pepper, minced
1 small onion, chopped
2 tablespoons each: rice vinegar
  and water
1 bay leaf
½ teaspoon Morton Lite Salt® Mixture
  Sugar substitute equal to 2 teaspoons
  sugar (i.e., 1 packet Equal®), or more
  to taste

In a covered saucepan, simmer peppers, onion, vinegar, water, bay leaf and Morton Lite Salt® Mixture until peppers are soft, about 15 minutes. Remove from heat and let cool. Remove bay leaf, and add sugar substitute. Refrigerate for up to 4 days. Serves 8 (3 tablespoons per serving).

Per serving: 9 cal. (8% from fat); 0.24 g protein; 0.08 g fat (0.01 g sat.); 2 g carbo.; 73 mg sodium; 0 mg chol.; 0.5 g fiber. Exchanges: Free for 2 servings.

Desserts

Lite Pumpkin Pie

A low-fat version of a favorite holiday treat.

2 cups canned pumpkin
2 cups water
1 cup low-fat (½% fat) milk powder
  (equal to 4 cups low-fat milk)
2 eggs
  Sugar substitute equal to ¾ cup brown
  sugar (i.e., ¾ cup Brown SugarTwin®)
½ teaspoon Morton Lite Salt® Mixture
1 teaspoon ground cinnamon
½ teaspoon each: ground ginger, nutmeg
  and allspice
¼ teaspoon ground cloves

Mix all ingredients. Pour into a 9" glass pie pan sprayed with nonstick spray. Bake in a preheated 350° oven for 1 hour, or until knife inserted in center of pie comes out clean. Serves 6.

Per serving: 114 cal. (23% from fat); 8.3 g protein; 2.9 g fat (1.3 g sat.); 14.6 g carbo.; 203 mg sodium; 76 mg chol.; 1 g fiber. Exchanges: 1 vegetable, ¾ low-fat milk.

Cherry-Topped Cheesecake

A rich-tasting, elegant dessert.

1 cup wheat nuggets cereal, pulverized in
  blender or food processor
3 envelopes unflavored gelatin
1½ cups water, divided
2 tablespoons vanilla extract
2 teaspoons almond extract
  Sugar substitute equal to ¾ cup sugar
  (i.e., 18 packets Equal®)
1 can (20 oz.) "lite" cherry pie filling or
  water-packed sweet cherries with juice
4 cups low-fat (2% fat) cottage cheese

Coat a 9" springform pan (or a deep-dish 10" pie pan) with nonstick spray. Pour in pulverized cereal, turning pan so that cereal sticks to the sides of the pan. Let remaining cereal settle to the bottom of the pan and smooth so that it becomes an even bottom crust. Mix gelatin with ¾ cup water in a heat-proof glass measuring cup. Let soften for 2 minutes. Heat in a microwave oven for 1 minute, or until hot. Stir to dissolve. Add ¾ cup cool water, vanilla, almond extract and sugar substitute. Mix ⅓ of gelatin mixture with cherries, then chill in refrigerator. Mix remaining gelatin mixture with cottage cheese in a blender or food processor. Pour the cheese mixture over the cereal crust and refrigerate. When the cheese mixture has begun to set up, but before the cherry mixture is firmly set, pour the cherry mixture over the cheese mixture. Refrigerate for several hours before serving. Serves 10.

Per serving: 145 cal. (6% from fat); 14.2 g protein; 0.92 g fat (0.56 g sat.); 20 g carbo.; 379 mg sodium; 4 mg chol.; 0.8 g fiber. Exchanges: 2 lean meat, ½ bread, ⅔ fruit. Add 1 fat exchange to meal plan.

Chocolate Cheesecake

Serve with a dollop of "lite" whipped topping.

1 cup wheat nuggets cereal, pulverized in blender or food processor
⅔ cup water
3 tablespoons vanilla extract
⅓ cup flour
¼ cup unsweetened cocoa powder
Sugar substitute equal to 1 cup sugar (i.e., 24 packets Equal®)
4 cups low-fat (2% fat) cottage cheese

Coat a 9" springform pan (or a deep-dish 10" pie pan) with nonstick spray. Pour in pulverized cereal, turning pan so that cereal sticks to the sides of the pan. Let remaining cereal settle to the bottom of the pan and smooth so that it becomes an even bottom crust. In a food processor or blender, mix water, vanilla, flour, cocoa and sugar substitute; add cottage cheese and mix until smooth. (If using a blender, divide ingredients into 2 batches for easier handling.) Pour over crumb crust in pan and bake in a preheated 300° oven for 1 hour. Chill thoroughly in refrigerator before serving. Serves 8.

Per serving: 205 cal. (19% from fat); 20 g protein; 4.3 g fat (1.7 g sat.); 25.7 g carbo.; 521 mg sodium; 10 mg chol.; 1.14 g fiber. Exchanges: 2 lean meat, 1½ bread.

Key Lime Cheesecake

Instead of lime, any sugar-free gelatin flavor may be used.

1 cup wheat nuggets cereal, pulverized in blender or food processor
1 package (0.6 oz.) lime-flavored sugar-free gelatin mix
1½ cups boiling water
1 tablespoon finely grated lime rind, optional
Sugar substitute equal to ¼ cup sugar (i.e., 6 packets Equal®)
6 cups low-fat (2% fat) cottage cheese

Coat a 9" springform (or a deep-dish 10" pie pan) with nonstick spray. Pour in pulverized cereal, turning pan so that cereal sticks to the sides of the pan. Let remaining cereal settle to the bottom of the pan and smooth so that it becomes an even bottom crust. In a heat-proof bowl, stir boiling water and gelatin mix until completely dissolved. Let cool at room temperature. (Do not chill.) In a food processor or blender, thoroughly mix cooled, dissolved gelatin, lime rind (if used), sugar substitute and cottage cheese. (If using a blender, divide ingredients into 3 batches for easier handling.) Pour cheesecake mixture over crumb crust. Smooth top, then refrigerate several hours before serving. Serves 12.

Per serving: 133 cal. (15% from fat); 17 g protein; 2.2 g fat (1.4 g sat.); 12 g carbo.; 503 mg sodium; 9 mg chol.; 0.67 g fiber. Exchanges: 2 low-fat milk, 1 bread. Add ½ fat exchange to meal plan.

Pumpkin Spice Cake

This moist cake is delicious with Creamy Vanilla Frosting (recipe below).

1¼ cups each: unbleached and whole wheat flour
1 tablespoon baking powder
1 teaspoon baking soda
1½ teaspoons ground cinnamon
½ teaspoon ground cloves
Sugar substitute equal to ½ cup brown sugar (i.e., ½ cup Brown SugarTwin®)
2 eggs
1½ cups nonfat milk
2 tablespoons canola oil
3 tablespoons honey (or an equivalent amount of sugar substitute, i.e., 3 tablespoons Brown SugarTwin®)
1½ cups canned plain pumpkin
1 tablespoon finely grated orange rind
½ cup raisins
½ cup chopped walnuts, optional
1 medium unpeeled apple, coarsely grated (or substitute ½ cup canned plain pumpkin)

In a large mixing bowl, mix flours, baking powder, baking soda, cinnamon, cloves and sugar substitute. In a blender, mix eggs, milk, oil, honey, pumpkin and orange rind. Add to flour mixture with raisins, nuts (if used) and grated apple. Stir to mix. Pour into a 9" by 13" baking dish sprayed with nonstick spray. Bake in a preheated 400° oven for 20 to 25 minutes, or until toothpick inserted in center comes out clean. Serves 20.

Per serving: 108 cal. (18% from fat); 3.34 g protein; 2.2 g fat (0.34 g sat.); 19.5 g carbo.; 123 mg sodium; 21.6 mg chol.; 1.73 g fiber. Exchanges: 1 bread, ½ fat.

Creamy Vanilla Frosting

For variety, any sugar-free instant pudding flavor may be used.

1 package (1.5 oz.) sugar-free instant vanilla pudding mix
2 cups nonfat milk
8 ounces "lite" whipped topping

Stir pudding mix and milk for 1 minute with an electric mixer. Using a spatula, gently fold in whipped topping. Makes 20 servings. (Note: Makes enough frosting for tops of two 8" or 9" round layers or one 9" by 13" cake.)

Per serving: 54 cal. (55% from fat); 3.8 g protein; 3.3 g fat (0 g sat.); 5.6 g carbo.; 50 mg sodium; 0 mg chol.; 0 g fiber. Exchanges: ½ low-fat milk.

Carrot-Raisin Cake

Serve with Creamy Vanilla Frosting (see p. 126).

½ cup each: unbleached and whole wheat flour
1 teaspoon each: baking powder and ground cinnamon
½ teaspoon baking soda
1 package (3 tablespoons) Butter Buds® Sugar substitute equal to ¾ cup brown sugar (i.e., ¾ cup Brown SugarTwin®)
1 cup medium-grated carrot
⅓ cup raisins
1 egg, beaten
¾ cup water

Mix dry ingredients, then add carrot and raisins. Next add egg and water. Stir only until mixed. Pour batter into an 8" square baking pan sprayed with nonstick spray. Bake in a preheated 350° oven for 20 to 25 minutes, or until toothpick inserted in center comes out clean. Serves 10.

Per serving: 73 cal. (8% from fat); 2.1 g protein; 0.65 g fat (0.19 g sat.); 15.2 g carbo.; 145 mg sodium; 21.3 mg chol.; 0.77 g fiber. Exchanges: 1 bread.

Applesauce-Raisin Cookies

The brown sugar flavor is sure to please!

1 cup each: unbleached and whole wheat flour
3½ cups uncooked oats, quick or old-fashioned
1 tablespoon baking powder
1 teaspoon baking soda
1½ teaspoons ground cinnamon
½ teaspoon each: ground nutmeg and ground allspice
¼ teaspoon cream of tartar
1 package (3 tablespoons) Butter Buds® Sugar substitute equal to ⅔ cup brown sugar (i.e., ⅔ cup Brown SugarTwin®)
½ cup raisins
2 eggs
2⅔ cups unsweetened applesauce
½ cup water
1 tablespoon vanilla extract

Mix flours, oats, baking powder and soda, cinnamon, nutmeg, allspice, cream of tartar, Butter Buds®, sugar substitute and raisins. In a blender, mix eggs, applesauce, water and vanilla. Add to flour mixture and stir until mixed. Drop by the tablespoonful onto 2 cookie sheets sprayed with nonstick spray and bake in a preheated 375° oven for 15 minutes. Makes 48 cookies.

Per cookie: 52 cal. (12% from fat); 1.66 g protein; 0.69 g fat (0.08 g sat.); 10.4 g carbo.; 47 mg sodium; 8.9 mg chol.; 0.32 g fiber. Exchanges: ⅔ bread.

Persimmon-Applesauce Cookies

These moist cookies freeze very well.

3½ cups pureed persimmon pulp
3½ cups unsweetened applesauce
3   eggs
3   cups water
    Sugar substitute equal to 3 cups brown
    sugar (i.e., 3 cups Brown SugarTwin®)
6   cups uncooked oats, quick or
    old-fashioned
3   cups each: unbleached flour and whole
    wheat flour
2   tablespoons baking soda
1   tablespoon baking powder
1½ tablespoons ground cinnamon
1   teaspoon each: ground nutmeg and
    ground allspice
1   cup raisins
1   cup chopped walnuts, optional

Mix persimmon pulp, applesauce, eggs and water. In a large mixing bowl, mix sugar substitute, oats, flours, baking soda and powder, spices, raisins and nuts (if used). Stir in applesauce mixture. Spray 2 cookie sheets with nonstick spray. Drop batter by the tablespoonful onto cookie sheets. Bake in a preheated 375° oven for 20 minutes. Switch the top sheet to a lower oven shelf and the bottom sheet to an upper oven shelf. Bake for 20 minutes longer. Remove from oven. Bake remaining batter in the same manner. Makes 72 cookies.

Per cookie: 79 cal. (10% from fat); 2.7 g protein; 0.87 g fat (0.09 g sat.); 16 g carbo.; 90 mg sodium; 8.9 mg chol.; 0.95 g fiber. Exchanges: 1 bread.

Apple-Raisin Bars

A wholesome snack for the entire family.

¾ cup whole wheat flour
1 tablespoon baking powder
1 teaspoon ground cinnamon
   Sugar substitute equal to ¼ cup sugar
   (i.e., ¼ cup SugarTwin®)
4 medium apples (unpeeled),
   coarsely grated
2 cups cold cooked rice
¼ cup each: shredded dried coconut
   and raisins
2 eggs, beaten

In a large mixing bowl, mix flour with baking powder, cinnamon and sugar substitute. Mix in remaining ingredients. Pour into a 9" by 13" baking pan sprayed with nonstick spray and bake in a preheated 325° oven for 40 minutes. Makes 20 bars.

Per bar: 77 cal. (13% from fat); 1.9 g protein; 1.15 g fat (0.57 g sat.); 15.2 g carbo.; 75 mg sodium; 21.3 mg chol.; 1.4 g fiber. Exchanges: 1 bread.

Brownies with Mocha Frosting

A chocolate dream come true.

Brownies:
- 2 cups unbleached flour
- ¼ cup unsweetened cocoa powder
- ¼ teaspoon Morton Lite Salt® Mixture
- 1½ tablespoons Butter Buds®
  Sugar substitute equal to 1 cup brown sugar (i.e., 1 cup Brown SugarTwin®)
- ½ cup water
- 1 cup low-fat (1% fat) buttermilk
- ½ cup unsweetened applesauce
- 1 tablespoon canola oil
- 2 teaspoons vanilla extract
- 1 teaspoon baking soda
- 2 eggs

Frosting:
- 1 envelope unflavored gelatin, mixed in ¼ cup water (to soften gelatin)
- ⅓ cup boiling water
- 2 tablespoons unsweetened cocoa powder
- 1 cup low-fat (½% fat) milk powder, equal to 4 cups low-fat milk
- 1 tablespoon vanilla
- 1½ teaspoons instant coffee powder, regular or decaf
  Sugar substitute equal to ⅝ cup sugar (i.e., 15 packets Equal®)
- 3 tablespoons chopped walnuts, optional

Brownies: In a mixing bowl, combine flour, cocoa, Morton Lite Salt® Mixture, Butter Buds® and sugar substitute. In a blender, mix water, buttermilk, applesauce, oil, vanilla, baking soda and eggs. Pour over flour mixture, then stir to mix. Pour batter into a 9" by 13" baking pan sprayed with nonstick spray. Bake in a preheated 350° oven for 15 to 20 minutes, or until a toothpick inserted in center comes out clean. Let brownies cool before adding frosting.

Frosting: Dissolve softened gelatin by mixing with boiling water. Pour into a blender and add cocoa, milk powder, vanilla, coffee powder and sugar substitute. Mix until blended. Refrigerate until moderately thickened (yet spreadable), about 10 minutes.

Spread frosting over cooled, uncut brownies in pan. Top with chopped nuts (if used). Refrigerate for at least 1 hour before serving, to allow frosting to become firm. Serves 20.

Per serving: 95 cal. (16% from fat); 4.25 g protein; 1.7 g fat (0.63 g sat.); 15.8 g carbo.; 118 mg sodium; 23.5 mg chol.; 0.36 g fiber. Exchanges: 1 bread.

Chocolate Sauce

Rich, chocolaty and satisfying!

- 3 tablespoons unsweetened cocoa powder
- 4 teaspoons cornstarch
- 1½ cups nonfat milk
- 1 tablespoon vanilla extract
- 1½ teaspoons maple-flavored extract
  Sugar substitute equal to 1½ cups sugar (i.e., 36 packets Equal®)

Stir together cocoa, cornstarch and nonfat milk to blend in a small saucepan. Cook over medium heat, stirring constantly, until thickened. Remove from heat and stir in vanilla, maple extract and sugar substitute. Chill before serving. Serves 12 (2 tablespoons per serving).

Per serving: 18 cal. (5% from fat); 1.27 g protein; 0.09 g fat (0.05 g sat.); 3.1 g carbo.; 25 mg sodium; 1 mg chol.; 0 g fiber. Exchanges: Free for one serving.

Raisin-Bread Pudding

This is a delicious dessert, snack or breakfast treat.

3 cups nonfat milk
2 eggs
Sugar substitute equal to ⅓ cup sugar (i.e., ⅓ cup SugarTwin®)
1 teaspoon vanilla extract
4 slices white bread, cubed
¼ cup raisins
1 teaspoon finely grated orange or lemon rind, optional

In a blender, mix milk, eggs, sugar substitute and vanilla. Mix bread cubes, raisins and rind (if used) in a bowl. Pour milk mixture over bread mixture and stir until blended. Pour into a medium-sized casserole dish sprayed with nonstick spray. Set this casserole in a pan with 1" of hot water. Bake in a preheated 350° oven for 40 to 50 minutes, or until a knife inserted in center comes out clean. Serves 6.

Per serving: 141 cal. (17% from fat); 9 g protein; 2.6 g fat (0.8 g sat.); 20.8 g carbo.; 166 mg sodium; 73 mg chol.; 0.9 g fiber. Exchanges: 1 bread, ½ nonfat milk, ½ fat.

Old-Fashioned Baked Custard

A creamy, rich-tasting dessert.

2 cups low-fat (1% fat) milk
2 eggs
⅛ teaspoon each: Morton Lite Salt® Mixture and ground nutmeg
Sugar substitute equal to ⅓ cup sugar (i.e., ⅓ cup SugarTwin®)
1 teaspoon vanilla extract

Mix all ingredients in a blender, then pour into 1 medium-sized casserole or 5 individual casseroles, sprayed with nonstick spray. Set casserole(s) in a larger, shallow pan containing 1" hot water. Bake in a preheated 325° oven for 1 hour, or until knife inserted near edge of custard comes out clean. Let cool briefly, then refrigerate. Serves 5.

Per serving: 77 cal. (36% from fat); 5.7 g protein; 3.04 g fat (1.26 g sat.); 6.5 g carbo.; 103 mg sodium; 89 mg chol.; 0 g fiber. Exchanges: ½ low-fat milk.

Easy Rice Pudding

Quick to fix and sure to please!

1 cup short grain rice
2 cups water
4 cups nonfat milk
1 package (1.2 oz.) sugar-free vanilla pudding mix (cooking type, not instant)
¼ teaspoon ground cinnamon
½ cup raisins

In a covered saucepan, simmer rice in water for 20 minutes, or until tender. In a blender, mix milk, pudding mix and cinnamon. Cook according to package directions until thick. Add to cooked rice. Add raisins and stir to mix. Serves 8.

Per serving: 182 cal. (9% from fat); 6 g protein; 1.74 g fat (0.09 g sat.); 35.4 g carbo.; 168 mg sodium; 0.5 mg chol.; 1.16 g fiber. Exchanges: 1 bread, ½ nonfat milk, 1 fruit.

Cinnamon Baked Apples

A healthy, sweet treat with lots of fiber.

4 medium apples, cored
½ teaspoon ground cinnamon
Sugar substitute equal to ¼ cup brown sugar (i.e., ¼ cup Brown SugarTwin®)
½ cup water

Cut the top ¼" off each apple, then place apples in a deep casserole dish. Sprinkle with cinnamon and sugar substitute. Add water and cover tightly with a lid or aluminum foil. Bake in a preheated 350° oven for 40 to 50 minutes, until apples are very tender. Serves 4.

Per serving: 89 cal. (5% from fat); 0.3 g protein; 0.5 g fat (0.1 g sat.); 23 g carbo.; 1 mg sodium; 0 mg chol.; 3.2 g fiber. Exchanges: 1½ fruit.

Apple Crisp

Serve warm for a fresh-baked flavor.

6 medium Golden Delicious apples, cored and cut into chunks
1 teaspoon ground cinnamon
Sugar substitute equal to ½ cup brown sugar (i.e., ½ cup Brown SugarTwin®)
2 cups water, divided
1 tablespoon cornstarch
2 cups fat-free granola with raisins

Place apple pieces in a medium-sized baking dish. Sprinkle with cinnamon and sugar substitute. Add 1 cup water. Cover tightly with aluminum foil and bake in a preheated 350° oven for 1½ hours. Remove from oven and add cornstarch dissolved in 1 cup water. Stir until thickened. Scatter granola with raisins over the top. Serves 6.

Per serving: 177 cal. (3% from fat); 2.8 g protein: 0.51 g fat (0.1 g sat.); 45 g carbo.; 13.6 mg sodium; 0 mg chol.; 6.2 g fiber. Exchanges: 1 bread, 2 fruit.

Wine-Poached Pears

The perfect finale to an excellent meal.

4 whole cloves
4 medium, ripe pears
½ cup each: red wine and water
1 2" piece cinnamon stick (or ½ teaspoon ground cinnamon)
1 teaspoon finely grated lemon rind
Sugar substitute equal to 3 tablespoons sugar (i.e., 3 tablespoons SugarTwin®)

Insert cloves at blossom end of each pear. Place pears in a saucepan with remaining ingredients. Cover and simmer for 15 minutes, or until tender. Remove pan from heat and let pears cool in liquid, then refrigerate. Serve chilled with poaching liquid. Serves 4.

Per serving: 123 cal. (5% from fat); 0.76 g protein; 0.7 g fat (0.04 g sat.); 26.3 g carbo.; 2.74 mg sodium; 0 mg chol.; 4 g fiber. Exchanges: 2 fruit.

Strawberry-Rhubarb Parfait

Colorful and full of flavor.

2 cups boiling water
1 package (0.6 oz.) strawberry-flavored
sugar-free gelatin mix
1¾ cups cold water
1 cup cooked, cubed rhubarb
½ cup "lite" whipped topping

In a large, heat-proof bowl, stir boiling water into gelatin mix until completely dissolved. Stir in cold water and rhubarb. Chill until slightly thickened. Stir again, then pour into 4 parfait glasses. Refrigerate until gelatin has completely set, then top each with 2 tablespoons whipped topping. Serves 4.

Per serving: 67 cal. (27% from fat); 4.1 g protein; 2 g fat (0 g sat.); 8.9 g carbo.; 101 mg sodium; 0 mg chol.; 0.35 g fiber. Exchanges: 2 vegetable, ½ fat.

Raspberry-Applesauce Treat

Great for dessert or a snack!

1 package (0.6 oz.) raspberry-flavored
sugar-free gelatin mix
2 cups boiling water
½ teaspoon ground cinnamon
1½ cups unsweetened applesauce
1 cup nonfat, sugar-free
vanilla-flavored yogurt
"Lite" whipped topping or additional
vanilla-flavored yogurt, optional

In a heat-proof bowl, stir boiling water into gelatin mix until completely dissolved. Measure 1½ cups. Add cinnamon and applesauce. Stir well, then pour into an 8" glass baking dish or 8 dessert glasses and refrigerate. Mix remaining gelatin with yogurt. Chill until slightly thickened, then spoon over gelatin in baking dish or glasses. Chill until set, about 3 hours. Garnish with whipped topping or yogurt, if desired. Serves 8.

Per serving: 42 cal. (1% from fat); 2.45 g protein; 0.04 g fat (0 g sat.); 7.2 g carbo.; 71 mg sodium; 0 mg chol.; 0.26 g fiber. Exchanges: ½ fruit.

Grape-Melon Medley

A light, refreshing dessert.

½ medium cantaloupe, cut into cubes
or balls
1 cup watermelon, cut into seedless
cubes or balls
1 cup small, seedless grapes
4 mint sprigs, optional

Mix cantaloupe, watermelon and grapes. Garnish each serving with a mint sprig, if desired. Serves 4.

Per serving: 51 cal. (8% from fat); 0.97 g protein; 0.47 g fat (0.07 g sat.); 12.4 g carbo.; 7 mg sodium; 0 mg chol.; 1.5 g fiber. Exchanges: 1 fruit.

Index

The titles of recipes are capitalized. Recipes are listed alphabetically, by title and by keywords in the title. Titles of ethnic recipes not beginning with name of country or region are listed geographically as well as by title. Recipes listed under "vegetarian dishes" contain no animal products; those under "lacto-vegetarian dishes" contain milk products; those under "ovo-vegetarian dishes" contain eggs; those under "lacto-ovo-vegetarian dishes" contain both milk products and eggs.

Suzi Castle

Syndicated health and cooking columnist Suzi Castle ("Cooking With Suzi") was born and educated in California, where she now lives, writes, and cooks. Surrounded by excellent chefs throughout her childhood, Suzi learned culinary creativity at an early age. Her extensive travels throughout the world have provided her with a strong background and interest in international cultures and cuisines, which she incorporates into her writing.

Raised in an artistic family, Suzi was encouraged to try various media. Her artistic background includes a one-person show of her water color paintings and illustrations, clay sculpture, and creative writing. She began her journalism career as food editor for the *San Juan Bautista Echo*. Through her syndicated weekly column she shares healthful cooking tips and recipes with a growing circulation of over half a million readers.

Suzi's first love, though, is the art of cooking. As she reveals in her book, "Cooking is a very satisfying art form, another way to express yourself creatively. Writing a health cookbook is the culmination of my long-time interest in combining cooking with living a healthy life-style."

Suzi Castle is an active member of the American Diabetes Association and The Mended Hearts, Inc., a support group for heart patients.

Dear Reader:

I welcome your comments and suggestions. Please write to me at the address below. To order additional copies of **SUZI CASTLE'S DELICIOUSLY HEALTHY FAVORITE FOODS COOKBOOK** — please send $14.95 per copy plus $2.50 postage and handling (and sales tax for CA residents).

HEALTH COOKBOOKS
Rt. 4, Box 208
Porterville, CA 93257-9708